BRAD PATTISON'S

puppy
book

A Step-by-Step Guide

to the First Year of Training

random house canada

PUBLISHED BY RANDOM HOUSE CANADA

Copyright © 2012 Brad Pattison

www.randomhouse.ca

Library and Archives Canada Cataloguing in Publication

Pattison, Brad
    Brad Pattison's puppy book : a step-by-step guide to the first year of training / Brad Pattison.

Includes index.
Issued also in electronic format.

ISBN 978-0-307-36097-7

    1. Puppies. 2. Puppies—Training. I. Title.

SF427.P38 2012   636.7'07   C2011-908143-1

Cover and text design by Terri Nimmo
Cover image: © Vicki Reid / istockphoto
Printed and bound in the United States of America

10 9 8 7 6 5 4 3 2 1

This book is dedicated to all puppies and
puppy owners who wholeheartedly
embrace the opportunity to embark on
an amazing journey together.

contents

introduction

*Expect success. Be surprised when your dog does
something wrong and breaks the canine laws,
not when your dog does something right.*

In my more than twenty years of training dogs and
studying canine behaviour, I've never known a dog
to respond negatively to consistent, sound guidance
and a home life based on mutual respect. My training methods and philosophies are geared toward
helping humans fully understand the canine point
of view and toward teaching people how to harness
their pup's needs, skills and traits to ensure harmony
within the interspecies pack. I don't think of puppy
training as something that should be done for a few
hours per week in a sterile classroom environment,
where the owner learns potentially dangerous gim-
micks like treat training or how to use an obedience
clicker. Not a chance. Training and bonding with
your dog are not about pigeonholing you and your
puppy or making you conform to a set of boring

rules; the process is ultimately about unleashing the potential of both species. I believe that every dog has great potential and that it's up to us humans to discover and nurture that capacity and also to learn from it. Positive dog training doesn't come from a place of fear and brute dominance; it's about empowering people with information and skills that harness and celebrate dogs' abilities.

Synchronizing our body language to "speak canine" actually means minimizing anxiety, fear, anger and doubt. We are the leaders, and that naturally means it's our job to safeguard our pups against hazards and to gain their trust by teaching them the rules of conduct in our human pack. It's also our responsibility to streetproof them so they can safely enjoy off-leash freedom. The ultimate goal is to give both species the fun and freedom they deserve and to take the bond to greater heights by embracing new challenges, activities and environments. It's about establishing and maintaining your dog's trust in you and trusting what your dog can do.

In this book, I'll show you how to recognize and work with your pup's needs, so you can harness all of your dog's wonderful skills, talents and traits and effectively communicate and bond with him. My role is to be your canine interpreter and to take you step by step through your puppy's first year, so you'll have a better understanding of what's happening between those fuzzy ears. This book offers in-depth explanations of a variety of tools and techniques for your own personalized dog-training toolbox. They're all designed to be highly interactive and adaptable to our busy human schedules, so you can carry them out in tandem with your day-to-day life. No boring classroom required. You'll never hear me barking, "Two hours of intensive training every single day for four weeks in a stuffy classroom!" That kind of sterile and downright artificial "obedience" training sucks the life, energy and fun out of the process.

My training strategies are built for the real world and should be mixed in with your daily activities, whether you're running errands, chauffeuring your kids around, cooling your heels at a café or chilling at home. It's about building confidence and respect for both you and your pup by tapping into the dog's innate desire to be a member of a structured, well-balanced pack. And I can't say it enough: when raising your puppy to become a well-behaved and contented member of your *human* pack, remember that you're raising a *dog* and that a dog is a pack animal with the skills and power of a predator near the top of the food chain.

I know there's no such thing as "one size fits all" when it comes to dog training, so unlike the approaches of many other trainers, my methods are rooted in interspecies communication. And once you understand how to tap into all of your pup's needs, you can tailor the tools and techniques to suit your situation. Take what you learn here and adapt it to the interactions between you and your pup. But remember that it's vital to be open minded, hard working and considerate of your pup's *canine* needs.

I'm not saying that the process is a stroll in the park. Puppies are very complex beings. Like us, they're all works in progress, learning about themselves and the world around them while we're learning about them. That's why it's so important to take advantage of every opportunity. Every single training and play session will help strengthen your interspecies bond, whether it happens during a long walk or whether it's sandwiched between buying groceries and getting back home to cook dinner. And it's especially important to capitalize on each stage of a puppy's development, particularly during the initial "imprinting" stage. Scientists say this stage spans the first sixteen weeks, but from my experience, I know there are imprinting opportunities throughout the pup's entire first year and beyond.

My promise to you is that if you are consistent and conscientious, this is the only dog book you will ever need to buy. My detailed, step-by-step advice and training techniques cover everything from establishing and maintaining your pack leadership and introducing household rules and boundaries to doing training exercises that will establish your pup's skill set and maintain a healthy lifestyle. I'll start off by guiding you through all the dos and don'ts of finding the ideal pup and outlining strategies for providing the ideal home environment. We'll then move on to bonding, initial house-training and sit-stay training before tackling my more advanced exercises, such as off-leash and urban agility training. With each step, I'll offer advice and tips for socializing with other dogs, pets and people and suggestions for fun and interactive techniques that will stimulate your pup's progressing physical and intellectual needs. Most important, along the way, I'll help you learn how to curb and modify some all-too-common *human* behaviours and mistakes that cause and amplify negative dog behaviours such as pulling at the leash, bolting, chewing, nipping, trashing your household possessions, jumping up, begging, excessive barking, separation anxiety and aggression. I'll teach you how to tap into your pup's point of view and raise an awesome dog companion.

Working on this book has been a real thrill for me because most of the time, I'm sought out as a dog trainer only *after* pups and dogs have developed negative behaviours and the entire human pack is already in chaos. Far too often, these dogs are in jeopardy of being dumped at an SPCA shelter, paying the ultimate price for negative *human* behaviours like impatience, doubt, anger, depression, anxiety, neglect, alienation and inconsistency—especially among couples and families who have become disconnected with each other or have other two-legged disharmonies. Dogs have made me a kinder and happier person, and my hope with this book is that by the end of your first year with your pup, you'll have established the ideal conditions to build a strong, positive bond. I guarantee that there will be both human and canine hiccups and errors, as well as emotional highs and lows as you earn each other's trust and respect, but I also know that your mutual efforts will pay off.

STAGE 1
what a puppy needs

Who doesn't love puppies? It's hard to believe that such adorable bundles of energy, curiosity and affection come in such tiny, angelic packages. You just want to eat them up! But within six months, a pup could eat *you* out of house and home if you're unwilling to commit fully to your role as caregiver: parent, teacher, coach, play buddy and student of canine behaviour. Suddenly, that innocent ball of fuzz could turn into a hound from hell and the fairy tale could morph into a nightmare, so it's crucial that within the first year, your pup is properly adapted into life with the human pack.

Are you are champing at the bit, ready to rush out and go shopping for a puppy? I understand your excitement, but before you start visiting shelters or meeting with breeders, I highly recommend that pet-owners-to-be take the time to do some pre-pet homework. Welcoming a four-legged friend into your family is a huge, life-changing commitment, and there are plenty of things to consider other than potential names! My philosophy is that if you commit to getting it right from the get-go and lay a strong, healthy foundation, raising a pup can be such a stellar experience for both species. But building the solid foundation will take a whole boatload of *your* energy, effort, time, self-discipline, consideration, consistency, patience and curiosity.

If it's a realistic option, I always recommend pre-pet counselling. I offer this service to my clients, and a number of other trainers and some shelter organizations also do this type of work. The goal is to get

BREED CREED

I recommend that you do your research on breeds to help find a good match for your personality and lifestyle, but keep in mind that dogs aren't mass-produced robots that come in select versions with patch upgrades. All puppies develop unique personalities, with their own skills, talents, quirks and interests, and far too often, they can be boxed in and limited by breed bias. Too much breed profiling can unnecessarily shape *our* attitudes and behaviours, and we're then at risk of projecting those attitudes and behaviours onto our four-legged friends. I've met so many dogs who have defied their breed's traits or broken the mould. And I've also met so many dogs just doing what their breed has done for thousands of years, *for us*—protecting, guarding, hunting, herding, retrieving—only to be denied and punished *by us* for using those skills. Remember your pup is a canine first and foremost, and whatever your personality and lifestyle, it's imperative that you have the patience, energy, flexibility and empathy to meet your pup's needs and let that unique personality emerge and shine.

you thinking about the many responsibilities of raising a puppy and to provide advice and tips to help you think through all the steps. Then you can make the right decision for you and your family. If that isn't something you can pull off, the next best thing is to grab a pen and paper (or a laptop!) and work your way through the following list. (It would be ideal to pass the list along to all the members of your household as well.) Be honest with yourself because this isn't a purse we're talking about, and an impulsive pet purchase could live up to twenty years, or more. Dez, my faithful Border collie–Australian heeler cross, lived until the ripe old age of twenty-two!

Consider these talking points a do-it-yourself counselling session:

Are You Puppy Material?

- What's your personality? Are you mellow and easygoing or wired-for-sound and always on the go? Are you a stickler for rules and planning or do you just go with the flow? Are you messy? Do you like organized chaos? Are you a party animal with tons of friends or more of the solitary type? Are you touchy-feely? patient? Do you like to try new things or are you a creature of habit? Take a moment to visualize how your personality might affect your day-to-day life with a puppy and make a list of the possible conflicts of interest, along with the types of compromises you will be willing to make in order to be a responsible pet owner.

- What kind of lifestyle do you lead? Are you physically active? What kind of extracurricular activities do you participate in? Puppies and dogs need constant stimulation and novelty in their lives, so the more balanced you are, the more balanced they will be. What are some things that you already do that a puppy can do with you? (If you have mobility issues or are unwilling to provide your dog with lots of physical activities, consider adopting a senior dog that has started slowing down and will therefore be more than happy with daily, leisurely walks.)

- What's your daily schedule? Do you travel a lot for work? Chalk up a lot of overtime? Are you beholden to a strict routine? Take into account your work/life balance and be honest with yourself about the amount of time you can truly commit to training a puppy. Also record how you will adjust your life to suit a puppy's needs. If your daytimer is already jam-packed, it's doubtful that you'll be able to provide the ample time, energy, consistency, patience and *joie de vivre* needed to raise a pup. Is there anything you'd be willing to sacrifice? I'm a firm believer that dogs shouldn't be fixed to a strict schedule; it's not only a dull grind, but if they're put in a strict routine and you happen to deviate from that routine even once, they might act up by trashing the house. Just like us, dogs respond acutely to the element of surprise: in training, in exercise, and in their social lives.

- Are you (or anyone in your household) able to take some time off from work to be with your puppy for the first few days? How about the ability to take a puppy to work? During your pup's first days and months in your household, you'll need to spend as much time as possible getting to know her, monitoring behaviours, tending to house-training (meaning, potentially, a few days to a few weeks of disrupted sleep), bonding and playing chew games (among others). There's a huge time commitment for everyone involved, and if you don't carve out a place in your schedule for your pup now, you'll pay for it big time in the future.

- How many people make up your household? Is everyone willing to commit to the new pup? Not only for daily caregiving, but also by being consistent and working from the exact same page in terms of house rules and training? Consistency is key. I can't say it enough.

- Do you see your current living situation changing in the next month to year? marriage? a new baby? If you're planning to introduce a new member to your family within the next year, consider holding off on the pup until you've settled into your new situation, ideally waiting until your youngest child is three years of age unless you are 10,000,000 percent committed to devoting a large portion of your life to pup- and child-rearing. Puppies are keenly tuned in to body language, so any awkward movements are unnatural to them and could be perceived as threatening or weak. If your older children are begging for a pup, first get them to commit to taking good care of a plant or a goldfish for at least six months. Then set up play dates and even dog-training dates with well-balanced, mature dogs, so they come to understand the level of work, patience and consistency required before the pup enters their lives.

- Do you currently have a dog, a cat or other pets in your home? If you live in a multi-pet household, you probably already know how your pets react to other dogs and pups. An older dog can provide excellent guidance and support, but I suggest holding off on introducing a new pup to the family until your current dog is three years old — the point when dogs reach full maturity, understand the house rules and are able to provide guidance and structure to a new sibling. A well-behaved, contented adult dog can be a stellar teacher for your pup because she can tutor in a dog's natural language, speaking primarily through body language and movement and vocalizing largely through growling and only the occasional bark. It's even better if the dog you already have is five or six years old — or even in the golden senior years. But note that a pup should not be introduced to an elderly dog that has an aggressive streak or serious health issues.

- Where do you live? Do you live in an apartment or in a house with a backyard? Are you within walking distance of more than one dog park? I've said it before and I'll say it again: a backyard is just

DOUBLE TROUBLE

If you already have a dog and you're thinking about introducing a new pup to the pack, don't even consider it unless your current dog is a healthy and well-balanced member of the family. If your dog has behaviour issues, bringing in another dog, especially a wired and demanding pup, can actually intensify your dog's issues. Ditto for getting two pups at the same time, especially if they're from the same litter. Please remember that two puppies are often double trouble, creating more mischief, chaos and damage. If you already have household pets, you should know their strengths and limitations, so please introduce a pup to the mix only when you know your dog and your other pets can tolerate a boisterous pup.

a more spacious jail cell for your pup than a small indoor space, and it shouldn't become a substitute for long walks and romps. And you'll need to house-train your pup outside—no puppy pads, no little boxes, no newspapers! House-training is the only situation in which a designated backyard spot will come in handy during the initial few months, though urban dwellers can always find a patch of grass nearby. Are you willing to commit to providing your pup with lots of fresh air, exercise and socialization in a variety of places?

- Are you planning to move within the next year? Moving house is one of the most stressful events in *our* lives, and too often, we pass that stress onto our dogs, especially if we don't make the time to meet their doggy needs—even if those needs are ignored for only a brief period of time. Would you be willing to wait until you've settled into your new place before you bring a puppy into your life?

- Can you afford a puppy? And more important, can you afford a dog for the next twelve to sixteen years? Dogs can be very expensive, and it's your duty to provide adequate veterinary care, food, equipment and personal supplies, and perhaps also cash for grooming and pet sitting. Have you looked into pet health insurance?

- Are you happy and content with your life right now? I don't expect you and your life to be perfect. In my books, flaws and quirks, setbacks and mistakes are part and parcel of a well-balanced and meaningful life. However, even though dogs are amazing companions, a pup shouldn't be sentenced to fill a gaping void in your life. If you saddle your puppy with unrealistic expectations, especially uniquely human ones that are impossible for her to realize, you're probably in for a whole lot of trouble. If you've recently lost a companion—canine, human or otherwise—please don't rush the grieving process by getting a new pup. It's not fair to either species.

- This is by far the most important question of all: Are you prepared to become the pack leader? And I don't just mean picking up the torch where the pup's canine parent left off. You'll also have to take on the role of the dog's siblings. Those are a lot of paws to fill, and you have to be realistic

Winter, Spring, Summer or Fall?

You should also consider the ideal time of year to bring a pup into your life. If you live in Canada, the northern U.S. or Western Europe, it's best if your pup spends his first months with you during late spring or early summer. This gives you a good chunk of time to enjoy training and bonding with your pup outdoors before the winter season begins. For those of you living in hot climates, consider starting the process during the cooler, early winter months.

about whether you can take on all this responsibility for the animal's entire life. Think about the big picture.

Providing For Your Pup's Basic Canine Needs

Since your prospective pup can't read and sign a legal document before she becomes a part of your family, I'm going to take a moment and speak on her behalf by providing you with a list of primary concerns and expectations from her point of view. If you sign off on the following canine needs and then shirk your contractual obligations, you will pay for it in a huge way—sacrificing your family's peace of mind and potentially even your pup's life.

Your Puppy Pact shall include, but not be limited to, the following:

- Membership in an organized and healthy pack. This means being a well-behaved pack follower. For this to happen, you will need to consistently and patiently teach her the skills, rules and boundaries of the *human* pack, so she learns to be accountable for her behaviour and realizes that if she crosses those boundaries, her behaviours will be corrected.

- Daily physical exercise and the opportunity to follow her nose (to pick up the daily news of scents left behind by other animals), to add her own byline to the mix by leaving her own scent marks behind (primarily through elimination— urination and defecation) and to explore the sights, sounds and smells of new environments. As she matures and craves more freedom, she'll also need to be given the opportunity to venture off-leash.

- Socialization with other people and especially a variety of other dogs.

- Mental stimulation that will allow your pup to develop a sense of purpose in life.

- A healthy, well-balanced diet of dog food—not human food or dog treats.

- A comfortable area to call her own, where she can sleep and chill out.

- Three toys for playtime and also to prevent teeth- ing and chewing issues.

- A few basic grooming aids to maintain a healthy appearance.

- Loads of play, bonding and *dog-friendly* affection, primarily in the form of satisfying the doggy needs mentioned above—not human-centric affection like coddling and baby talk.

- The ability to express herself and be understood in dogspeak. (To understand "dogspeak," you will need to learn how to interpret and respect your pup's primary methods of communication: primarily via scent and visual sight (body language, movements and physical gestures) and secondarily by touch (praise and affection, mostly through grooming, massage techniques and play) and "speaking" (barking, growling, yelping).

Dogs Are Pack Animals, Not Sherpas

Remember that while dogs are pack animals, they're not meant to literally *pack* around our psychological baggage and live up to unrealistic, fairy-tale-like expectations. Far too often, we heap masses of complex *human* expectations and ideals onto our dogs. Before even shaking paws with that new buddy, many humans saddle him with piles of their own human baggage, and this only sets dogs up for failure. It's really important to have expectations for our pups, such as the ability to follow the basic rules of our domestic pack (being house-trained and obeying basic rules, for instance). But it's imperative that we differentiate our expectations about dogs from *human* desires, which are very complicated and nuanced and often downright impossible for canines to get their furry heads around.

Humans are pack animals too. The two species have flourished both independently and as mixed packs by cooperating with each other and living together not only for the sake of survival, but also to feed other important needs, like mental stimulation, empathy and what we call affection and love. Dogs meet these needs through play, grooming and parent–pup nurturing.

The domestic dog sees us as his pack family, and he's programmed, through evolution, to want to fit into our pack, however weird or chaotic it might be. So it's no surprise to me that dogs can get really confused—and sometimes downright trashed—when they fall into a pack that heaps too much human emotion onto them. These stresses hamper and often cripple all aspects of a dog's innate traits, making it impossible for that dog to be a functional member of the family pack—and far less an awesome and unique individual.

People wreak havoc on their pups and dogs by anthropomorphizing them (seeing their characteristics as human traits) or treating them like surrogate human partners. If you treat your pup like a human baby, you'll disrespect and neglect her unique canine needs and also potentially saddle your pup with a condition called "learned helplessness." And when you teach your pup to be helpless, all sorts of issues will come up, including insecurity, anxiety, depression and even aggression. In a nutshell, babying your dog smothers her potential to evolve and mature.

But as I'll discuss in this book, dogs are a lot like us in that they crave structure, communication, socialization, a sense of purpose in life, freedom and independence, whether they live in a wild pack or a human pack. Like us, they need boundaries and rules. As humans, we constantly juggle the desire for independence and autonomy with our need to have friends and loved ones. And we don't always act on our desire to loaf on the beach because we need to fulfill commitments and responsibilities. We have to work and pay the bills. Life is a fine balance, for us and for dogs.

For all of these reasons, I will occasionally compare a pup's developmental stages to specific human evolutionary stages. I'll call the seven- to nine-month period "the terrible twos," for instance, because so many canine traits during this phase—tantrums, meltdowns and constant pushing of boundaries—match the behaviours of a human two-year-old. And I'll compare the nine- to ten-month period to human adolescence because at this age, pups start to act like space cadets and also crave a fine balance of freedom and independence, along with the need for your respect and guidance. I have some reservations about using these human-like descriptions, but I've found that tapping into our own life experiences drives home the reality of the pup's point of view. The human analogy also demonstrates that, like us, dogs are smart, caring, curious, intellectually engaged, evolving pack members. They have their own unique skills, traits and needs that must be fostered, encouraged, respected and celebrated.

The role of memory is also important with dogs, just as it is with humans. It plays an important role both in their lives in general and during the training process. But one of the greatest canine traits is that dogs, for the most part, operate in the here and now. If dogs kept daytimers, their to-do lists would include all the basic forms of mental and physical stimulation, with a huge asterisk beside "be a good member of the family pack."

Dogs are usually more than willing and able to work and commit to us, but they don't have the opportunity to choose between being a wild dog or a domestic dog. And domestic dogs depend on us to give them enough freedom and autonomy. Just as we have dogs to fulfill our needs, we must never forget our dogs' needs.

Breed Compatibility

As I mentioned earlier, breed traits give you a great outline of some general breed characteristics, but every dog has her own unique personality, formed by a mix of nature and nurture. Though it's important to take all breed-related characteristics into consideration, remember that the way you raise your pet can have just as much influence on his ultimate personality and behaviour as the traits he had at birth. You might want a Border Collie because you visit your family farm every summer and love the focus and doggy work ethic of this breed, but not every Border Collie is inclined to herd, and those who are can't switch it off just because they're destined to grow up in the 'burbs. You might want a Rottweiler or a German shepherd to protect you and your family, but I've met plenty of Rotties and shepherds who had no desire to guard or whose instincts landed

Breeding Victims

There's no national reporting system for animal abuse, but based on media data collected by Pet-Abuse,[1] which has a database of more than 17,000 cases since 2000, the lion's share of victims are dogs, with nearly 10,000 dog abuse cases. Over 7,500 of these dog victims—the overwhelming majority—are Pit Bulls. Ownership of these dogs is restricted in some states and provinces, and they are often depicted negatively, but they are the most victimized animal in the grim database. The most common type of abuse they noted was neglect and abandonment, followed by pet hoarding, dog-fighting and mutilation.

them in crate prisons as soon as they showed off those skills without the right guidance. Some friends of mine have a cottage at the lake and wanted a dog that would go swimming, but their Labrador will have nothing to do with water. Boxers are said to be great family dogs, but they have oodles of energy that can be taxing for busy people, and they need a heap of constant stimulation to maintain balance.

When it comes to breed profiling, perhaps one of the most misunderstood and underestimated of the dog breeds is the "toy class." This is a relatively new breed category misguidedly billed as "ideal apartment dogs" or, worse, even "purse dogs" or "cuddle dogs." That classification is a way for breeders to sell dogs to people who shouldn't have pets in the first place. It's a marketing tool to trick people into thinking these breeds make cute accessories. This is not true because they are still *dogs*. A full-grown Yorkshire terrier can weigh less than ten pounds, but the breed still needs tons of time outdoors, proper exercise and socialization. The Puppy Pact should be your go-to guide when it comes to basic canine needs, no matter what the size or characteristics of the breed you're looking at.

How Much is That Puppy in the Window?

It never ceases to amaze me that people will often devote more time to shopping for shoes or stereos than to learning about a dog that they plan to live with for about the next fifteen years . So I'm going to share some information and advice with you, hoping that you'll then be motivated to do your due diligence as you investigate potential breeders and shelters. Notice that I didn't mention puppy mills or pet stores. That's because far too many pet stores and most puppy mills breed dogs for profit, with little to no regard for their dogs' health or well-being. Repeat after me: "I promise to stay away from all puppy mills and most pet store pups." A puppy mill is a breeding operation that "mass produces" as many pups as possible at minimal cost and for maximum financial gain. Common problems with puppy mills and the pet shops that trade in

Brad's Beefs

I have a big issue with people who treat their dogs like babies, communicate with them in baby talk, dress them up like dolls and feed them human food or attempt to train them using so-called "treats." It's like they expect them to fill a void that only humans are capable of filling. Many people who engage in this kind of behaviour have the best intentions, but they don't understand the potential dangers of stifling or neglecting a dog's unique needs.

pups include inbreeding, overbreeding, substandard living conditions, neglect, lack of quality vet care, improper nutrition and even physical abuse. These factors cause a slew of health issues for dogs: behavioural disorders like aggression and separation anxiety, blindness, infections, viruses, parasites, anemia, bladder and bowel disorders . . . I could go on and on. In most cases, pups in pet stores have been yanked from the litter too early, long before the pup is eight weeks old and has had that crucial bonding and learning time with her mom and siblings. Sometimes puppies are taken from their litters when they are as young as five weeks old, and they can spend weeks in transit before they even get to a store. Even for professionals like me, not every dog separated from his canine mom before the age of eight weeks can be fixed.

I know there are many awesome breeders out there, but when you start looking for a puppy, you're still entering a world of "Let the buyer beware," and it's extremely important that you do your research. Puppy mills aren't technically illegal in Canada — the government doesn't legislate commercial breeders — and it's a multimillion-dollar industry. However, laws have been passed piecemeal by provincial and municipal authorities: Richmond, British Columbia, was the first community to institute a ban on the sale of puppies in pet shops in 2011, but in my opinion, that legislation has actually made the situation even worse — at least in the short term — because many of the irresponsible breeders have gone underground. Pet advocates and organizations have been lobbying for positive change and the amendment of the

Cruelty to Animals Bill for decades, but there are still no federal licensing requirements for commercial breeders, so we have no clue as to how many of these horrid puppy mills exist in Canada. I encourage you to check your own province or state's humane society for legislation or the lack thereof as early as possible, so you can be informed about issues in your region. And before you make a decision, do as much hands-on research as possible: visit prospective breeders and their vets and check their references. People love talking about their pets, so poll your dog-owning friends and colleagues and people walking their dogs in local parks about breeds and breeders.

Puppy Mills

In the U.S., large-scale puppy mills are licensed by the Department of Agriculture, but it's up to each state to enforce inspections. Some have recently made positive steps in the fight to curb the activities of puppy factories by introducing sweeping reforms like inspections and mandatory licensing.

Backyard Breeders

We've all seen the huge volumes of newspaper and Internet ads placed by backyard breeders. But unfortunately, this group happens to be one of the primary causes of pet overpopulation, abandoned dogs and dog euthanization. Sometimes the incentive is money—people think that selling puppies is a good way to make a quick buck—but many backyard breeders are simply ignorant about how difficult and dangerous it really is and they don't have the knowledge, resources or skills required to raise a healthy, happy litter.

Breeding dogs is not a part-time hobby that should be dabbled in lightly. It's not something you can do simply because you already own a great dog or because you successfully bred a litter once. To be a breeder, you need to be in it for the long haul. A good breeder will also understand that it's not appropriate to let just any breeds or mixes reproduce; they should be tested for all sorts of health-related and genetic issues. But most often, that doesn't happen. Even though the initial price tag for the pup will be much lower than for one born at a reputable breeder's, you'll end up paying a huge price in the form of high vet bills, unnecessary suffering for everyone in the family and even tragedies like serious dog bites and the dog's death.

To prevent these horror stories, avoid amateur breeders and make sure to have your pup spayed or neutered to avoid becoming an amateur breeder yourself.

Investigating Your Breeder

If you decide to get your puppy through a breeder, do a thorough interview first and make sure the breeder has an excellent reputation. Ask for references and check them. Remember that breeders are charged with caring for puppies for their first eight weeks on the planet, and their influence will deeply affect the dog you will be taking care of for the rest of his life—which could be upwards of fifteen years!

For a breeder Q&A and for information on meeting and interviewing the breeder on-site, take a look at my breeder questionnaire in the Resources section at the back of this book. The information will help you ask the right questions and flag any concerns so you can figure out whether you're dealing with a legitimate breeder before you get near a bunch of super-cute pups.

If you visit a breeder and become concerned with the breeder's methods, or, worse, if you end up face to face with an inhumane puppy mill breeder holding a bunch of dirty, skinny, shivering pups captive in segregated cages, don't let yourself get sucked into a pity purchase. I've rescued many pups and worked with rescue organizations, so I know that the passionate pursuit of freeing abused animals requires an educated team of individuals, and in worst-case scenarios, an investigative SPCA team. Don't be tempted to play the white knight. Remove yourself from the environment and call the SPCA and the Better Business Bureau a.s.a.p. Turn those rats in! I have a particular problem with bad breeders because I've had to try to clean up so many of their messes.

> ## The Truth About Cats and Dogs
>
> Every eight seconds, a dog or cat is euthanized in the U.S., resulting in four million deaths a year.[2] According to the Humane Society of the United States, many of these animals are the result of overbreeding because so many pet owners neglect to spay or neuter their four-legged companions.

It's a good sign if the breeder asks *you* questions. I once worked with a Yellow Lab named Murphy who was trained off-leash in four months. His owner, Stephanie, sank her heart and soul into training the dog, and the whole family participated. The cherry on top was that the breeding was perfect. Not surprisingly, given the quality of the dog, I learned that before Stephanie acquired the pup, the breeder had asked her what kind of training she would do and even inquired about who I was and what my training methods were. He was vigilant and checked all the boxes before he signed off on any puppy. Please do the same by interviewing your breeder closely, so you get off on the right foot and paw!

Don't Pity the Pound Dog

Another option is to adopt a puppy from a shelter or rescue organization. And it's true that there are hundreds of great dogs and pups-in-waiting lingering at shelters through no fault of their own. Dogs are most often abandoned for selfish and avoidable reasons: a move or time constraints, for instance. In fact, nine of the top ten reasons why people send dogs to a shelter involve human lifestyle issues and poor choices, so their former dogs may make excellent pets. There are exceptions, though, and here's a word of warning: not every dog is salvageable. Some are born bent out of shape thanks to inbreeding and negligent breeding practices at puppy mills. Others have been so neglected or poorly trained that they could be saved only after an enormous amount of work and commitment—much more than most families are willing or able to provide. I applaud the devotion of shelters and rescue organizations because they typically have to operate on shoestring budgets with meagre resources. But you have to think about what that could mean for pups, given that shelters often lack adequate indoor and outdoor space and rarely have enough employees and volunteers to give pups and dogs the canine and human socialization they need.

If you've made the decision to adopt a puppy from a shelter or rescue organization, be sure to ask the staff as many questions as possible about the puppy's history, but always be wary of caving in when you hear a dog's tragic tale. Many of my clients have similar stories about dogs they've "rescued," and they've said things like "In our home, there's plenty of love to go around." Sure, they have a lot of *human* love to go around, but that doesn't mean they're fully aware of a canine's basic needs—which is especially important when dealing with a potentially abused dog.

TRICKY TREATS

Fascinating studies have recently been published in behaviour science journals concerning optimal positive reinforcers, and they point to some very disturbing issues related to treat-trained dogs. One study done by U.S. researchers with American veterinaries[3] found that dogs who were fed "commercial treats" and human table scraps were more likely to be obese and diagnosed with hypothyroidism, hyperadrenocorticism, diabetes mellitus, pancreatitis, ruptured cruciate ligament, neoplasia, bladder cancer or mammary cancer—many of them diseases that can cause premature death.

Food Baits Impede Obedience

If the threat of obesity and disease isn't enough, treats are also shown to cause inattentiveness and lack of obedience among dogs in an experiment conducted by the Vienna-based Clever Dog Lab.[4] The scientists conducting this study used food baits in certain experiments and found that these dogs were much less likely to obey their owner's commands than dogs in the non-food experiments.

Whether you adopt a very young pup, an older pup or a mature dog from a shelter, there's a good chance that you'll have to start from square one. Unfortunately, dogs from shelters can't always be retrained, so they end up back where they started, and this just creates a revolving door of heartaches.

The First Eight Weeks

It is imperative that puppies stay with their canine pack for at least the first eight weeks of their lives. Why? Because they need their mothers. They rely on them to provide nutrient-packed milk and to keep warm and clean. Then, as the weeks pass and the pups start to walk, the canine mom establishes rules and boundaries to ensure that none of her pups wanders too far from the den. (This safeguards them against predators.) She also teaches them how to play and socialize with each other and calls foul on any negative behaviours, primarily through gentle but firm nudging, nipping and scruffing (picking the pups up by the scruff of their necks). But if one of her pups steps out of line, she might blow the proverbial whistle with a growl. She disciplines negative behaviours swiftly

TOYS FOR TRAINING

A Belgian research team turned the lens on military dog trainers and their dogs and found that the top-ranking team (and three other teams among the top nine) used toys to reward dogs during training.[5] The authors of the study concluded that while the use of toys among working dog trainers was uncommon, it "could help to diminish dogs' distraction," a state of mind that negatively impacted training and led to increased punishments and lower performance scores. They also pointed out that for dogs that enjoy chasing animals as "natural rewards," tug-and-retrieve games could be used as "motivationally equivalent rewards."

and even pins pups down to remind them in no uncertain terms that she's the pack boss.

These initial eight weeks are so very precious and important for pups because the time they spend with their canine pack not only helps to safeguard them against disease, but also has a positive impact on potential negative characteristics like separation anxiety and aggression. By the time a pup enters your home at eight or nine weeks of age, she's already been preprogrammed by nature *and* nurture to be a docile, calm and well-behaved member of the pack. She already knows not to poop and pee where she eats and not to stroll away from her pack. She comes to you open and willing and expecting you to teach her the rules and regulations of your human pack. She also expects consequences for any negative behaviours.

STAGE 2
puppy preparedness

Now that you've found an ideal pup and are closing in on his arrival, it's time to puppy-proof your home and set up an area for your new dog to chill out and sleep. Then you'll be heading off to buy all the supplies he'll need.

I encourage you to take five minutes to get down on all fours and tour your home from your pup's low-rider point of view. You might feel like a lunatic, but the goal is to understand how tantalizing your two-hundred-dollar running shoes, your favourite cashmere socks or that seductive roll of toilet paper might look to a mouthy, teething pup.

Things to Watch Out For

- Move all items like toys, crayons, pens, pencils, paper clips, pins, tacks and staples out of reach.

- Tuck away any wires from lamps and electronics, and make sure excess wires are well contained and hidden.

- Keep all electrical and electronic devices unplugged when not in use (if possible) to avoid accidental electrocution.

- Check for hanging drawstrings from draperies or blinds, and wind them around a nail or bracket— away from your pup's paws and teeth.

- Move indoor plants out of your pup's reach for now. (Pups have been known to treat indoor plants like litter boxes and snack bars—and plants are potentially poisonous.

- Ditto for garbage cans (especially in the bathroom) and laundry baskets that can easily be reached with a snout or paws.

- Put all medicines in a safe, closed cabinet.

- Keep bathroom doors closed to prevent your pup from getting at the toilet paper.

- Keep the doors to the laundry room, pantry and your children's bedrooms closed.

- Keep windows closed.

- Consider purchasing baby gates to block off any staircases or rooms without doors that you don't want your puppy to access.

- If you have a garage, make sure that any items toxic to your pup are placed out of reach, including fertilizers, cleaning agents and antifreeze.

- If you have a swimming pool or pond, make sure it is inaccessible to the pup. Even if your puppy can swim, he can't necessarily get out of a man-made water feature by himself.

- Check fencing for weak or broken areas where your puppy could escape. Lock fence gates.

- If possible, don't use any chemicals like fertilizers, pesticides or herbicides on the lawn in and around the puppy's outdoor space. If you have to use them, keep the pup off the lawn for at least forty-eight hours after application.

- If you have a cat, make sure the puppy doesn't have access to his litter box. Your pup *will* eat the poop!

The bottom line is this: don't leave *anything* on the floor that you aren't willing to sacrifice to your pup, particularly in the early stages, when she's teething and becoming accustomed to the rules of the household. Umbilical training (we'll get to this in Stage 4) will also help you safeguard your pup from harm and from developing bad habits. Meantime, this initial puppy-proofing will make the first few weeks with your new pet safer and more relaxed.

Puppy Food

Protein is the key ingredient in puppy food, and that's why I recommend choosing a good raw-food diet or a dry, crunchy *puppy* kibble, ideally one that's also raw food-based. Canned dog foods tend to contain a lot of water and lower amounts of protein, and most adult kibbles come in shapes and sizes that are too large and ungainly for a pup's small mouth. The greatest advantages of dry kibble are that it helps to maintain healthy teeth (but you should still be brushing them!) and to curb teething issues. I recommend buying smaller bags of food and switching up the types of protein you feed your pup so he doesn't get bored with the same old flavour. This will also help him get his palette accustomed to trying new things. As long as your dog isn't too picky, he can try chicken, lamb, elk, bison or beef.

Once your pup starts to chow down, you'll want to look out for potential allergies and digestive problems. Both of these are quite common, especially in designer crossbreeds. With food-sensitive dogs, raw-food diets are usually recommended, so talk to your vet about the dietary issues of your pup's breed. Many vets who take a holistic approach will give you tons of great advice, and some pet stores have well-educated owners and staff and sell high-quality raw dog food and dry kibble. Your choice of food will also depend on the size of your pup. For larger breeds, including Newfoundlanders, Great Pyrenees, Great Danes and mastiffs, I recommend switching from high-protein puppy food to lower-protein adult dog food by about the age of six months. High-protein diets accelerate bone growth in larger breed dogs—who are prone to joint problems—and some pet experts believe that this can cause problems with joints and bone structure. Water is also a vital part of your pet's diet, and it needs to be fresh. Please, please remember to change your pup's water at least twice a day.

Hazardous Foods

I don't recommend feeding your pup *any* human food. Not even a single table scrap, please. Some human foods are not only deadly to pups—even in small amounts; many are high in fat and salt and contain all sorts of ingredients and preservatives that we

DOG OBESITY: RARELY IN THE GENES

According to a study carried out by Australian vets, thirty percent of their dog clients were obese, and 97 percent of obesity cases were chalked up to the dog owners' choices in diet, exercise and attitudes.[6] In a related study, the Australian researchers compared the lifestyles and routines of *dog owners* who had dogs of an average weight for their breed to owners who had obese dogs.[7] The study found that owners of healthy-weight dogs tended to live in households with a lower mean number of people, gave treats significantly less frequently and exercised their dogs daily, compared to once a week on average for owners of overweight dogs. (These overweight pets were much more likely to be confined in a yard as a form of exercise.)

humans might be able to tolerate but pups can't. Here are some of the most common culprits that can cause severe effects: dairy products, caffeine, chocolate, onions, avocado, the seeds or pits of fruits, grapes, raisins, rhubarb leaves (note that these are also poisonous to humans!), tomatoes (especially the leaves and stems), Xylitol (an artificial sweetener used in many desserts, chewing gum, candy, breath mints and toothpaste). Cooked bones are also hazardous because they splinter easily, so give your pup only raw bones, but avoid fish bones (even raw) because they are small and sharp. It's usually best to get your raw bones from the butcher or grocery store, where they're often considerably less expensive than at a pet store.

Also be aware of the potential hazards of food-related items that could choke or smother your pup, such as aluminum foil, candy wrappers and those plastic rings on six-packs. Signs of poisoning can appear within half an hour to forty-eight hours and include increased heart rate, vomiting, restlessness, tremors, increased urination and thirst, seizures and coma.

Poison Patrol

Both my website (www. bradpattison.com) and your local SPCA site have full lists of foods that are toxic to dogs, so please print one out, put it on the fridge and do your best to make sure your pup is never exposed to these poisonous foods.

Essential Puppy Gear

These days I find it disturbing to see how many blinged-out dogs are strutting around. They may look impressive, but just because they're well dressed doesn't mean they're confident and well balanced. Please remember that your puppy is an *animal* first and foremost. Pups don't care about the latest fashion trends and status symbols. To truly pamper your pooch, you need to give him your time, your energy, your patience and your respect of his canine needs. Not a high-fashion collar.

Less is so much more when it comes to puppy supplies, so try to keep it simple. Besides food and a puppy-proofed home, you'll need only a few essential items: food bowls, a collar and leash, a bed and crate, toys, a few clothing items and a small puppy grooming kit.

Food Bowls

You'll need two bowls—nothing fancy is required—but designate one for food and one for water. If you plan to do a lot of outdoor hikes and activities with your pup, you can also buy collapsible water bowls that are easy to carry.

Collars

A good collar and leash are essential. They make up the lifeline between you and your pup when you're bonding and training or out for a stroll. (More on this later, when I tell you about umbilical training, sit-stay training, street safety training, leash interruption and correction techniques and off-leash training.) For a good number of my puppy- and dog-training techniques, a Martingale-style collar is needed. It's designed to tighten only when there's tension on the leash, so it's the best collar for training *and* daily walks. A basic collar doesn't give you the control you'll need to lead your pup, and face muzzles, prong, choke and pinch collars often end up being instruments of torture. I've met a lot of dogs who were damaged by these devices, so it's no wonder they developed extreme anxieties about being collared and leashed. I don't like harness collars because they're designed for sled dogs, which means they encourage pulling, and the last thing you want to train your domestic pup to do is pull on the leash. It's like putting her in the driver's seat when you're the one who needs to be in control.

Buy a collar that fits your pup right now, even though you'll probably have to purchase several new ones until your pup is full grown. Measure the circumference of your pet's neck to get the right fit.

The Martingale Collar

I was introduced to the Martingale design by a veterinarian in Vancouver. It was created for horse training and later adapted to dog-training because it fits securely and comfortably around the neck and tightens only when your canine bolts ahead of you—or when you need to focus your pup's attention with the leash-guided correction. The collar is made of flat nylon material with a small attached portion of chain link and mimics the action of a choke collar but does the work in a safer, gentler way. Like a choke collar, it prevents your dog from backing out of the collar and escaping, but unlike a choke collar, it won't actually choke your dog. When the leash is pulled, only the chain portion of the collar contracts, not enough to choke, but enough to allow the handler to

A Martingale collar should be fitted to the exact size of the dog's neck when it is in the closed position.

correct or gain better control of the animal.

I've designed a great quick-release Martingale collar called the Hustle Up™, it has strong metal loops and buckle clasps and is far superior to similar collars with plastic clasps that crack easily and break. (The collar comes in all breed sizes and is available online at www.bradpattison.com and through pet stores.) Unlike other collars, it will never slip off your pup's head. Keep in mind that the initial imprinting stage of your puppy's development is extremely important and my Hustle Up™ collar won't let you and your pup down as you go through this phase together.

Leashes

When it comes to leashes, length matters. A leash that's too short will stifle your pup's freedom and mobility, but one that's too long won't give you adequate control over his movement. So please steer clear of long leashes and extendable click-and-grow-style leashes. If your pooch ends up wandering at the end of a leash that's too long, he'll be in potential danger, especially when you're out walking on the streets.

I recommend a six-foot (or 1.8-metre) leash. Look for a nylon leash because they're very durable and also washable. It should be approximately three-quarters of an inch wide (or two centimetres). For pups who will grow to be heavier than thirty-five pounds (about fifteen kilograms), I suggest a width of one inch (two and a half centimetres).

Bedtime

Sleeping dogs need to lie in their own beds. Never let your pup sleep in your bed, in any human bed or on human furniture. These are *your* spaces, and your pup needs to know from day one that furniture is off limits. Consistency is key in your pup's life, so don't cave on this matter even once. Not even when your significant other is out of town or your kid begs to let the pup sleep with him. You'll only be giving in to suit your own human desires, not your pup's canine needs. Instead, create a space that's designated exclusively as your pup's area, so she has a private place to sleep and chill out. That space must include some sort of bedding area for sleeping and a spot to keep your pup's three toys—yes, just three (see the "Toys" section below). And keep in mind that the closer to the ground your pup's bed is, the more grounded she will be because a pup who sleeps up—on your bed or on the couch—will start to think she's part of the leadership of the pack. You might think I'm being a stickler, but I've also seen so many dogs develop serious territorial issues around beds and couches, and puppies are especially vulnerable to falling off furniture and breaking bones. Small-breed adult dogs can also easily suffer from spine or limb damage if they're constantly jumping off furniture. The best solution is to put a dog bed in your living space, a comfy spot to rest that's all her own. During the initial housetraining phase, though, she should spend the night in a crate in your bedroom. There's a mind-boggling selection of doggy beds on the market, so take your time choosing the one that's right for you and your pooch.

As in the case of real estate, location counts most when it comes to a dog bed. If your pup's sleeping accommodation is on carpet or hardwood, you won't need a lot of padding in the bed, but if it's on concrete, linoleum or tile, you'll need an adequate barrier against cold and moisture between the floor and the bottom of the bed. If your pooch sleeps in the basement or some other area where the temperature will be dipping below 60°F (about 16°C), consider a slightly elevated or well-insulated bed. Look for low-maintenance beds that are large enough to allow for a six-inch (fifteen-centimetre) buffer around your pup. And feel free to buy a bed large enough for your pup once he's full grown. Look for materials that can be washed regularly.

Crates

A crate is the best place for your dog to sleep at night—especially when she's a pup. Even if you'd eventually prefer to have her sleep in a dog bed, it's extremely important to at least acclimatize your pup to being in a crate when she is young. If she has a good, comfortable time sleeping in her crate at a young age, she'll be less likely to associate the object with potentially stressful events like going to the vet, the kennel or the cargo area of an airplane. She needs to recognize the crate as her own personal safe place, a spot where she can go to take five. Keep a washable cotton blanket inside the crate and put one or two of your pup's favourite toys in there as well. That will make the spot appealing. A crate should never be used as a disciplinary device. It should always be a safe haven for your pup—much like a canine den in the wild.

Size matters when it comes to crates. If the crate's too big, the pup will not only feel lost; he might also be tempted to create a toilet zone in it. And you don't want to live with cleaning up messes or covering up smells. Sure, mistakes will probably happen—especially in the first few months—but you don't want your pup to make it a habit. The crate should be big enough for your pup to lie down and turn around, and when he's sitting or standing he should have between three and five inches of extra head room. If you have a small-breed dog, his first crate might still be big enough once he reaches physical maturity, but for large-breed dogs, you'll probably need to scale up the crate size once, or even twice, as he grows. If expense is an issue, consider trading up to larger models or renting crates. You can buy, sell and trade crates online or ask around at vets' and pet stores for crate-trading programs.

Toys

Pups love their toys, and you can get a lot of joy from watching them bounding around with their playthings! But toys are about much more than just playtime. They're crucial to your pup's development and well-being. They make teething time easier, and they fend off behavioural problems. They strengthen your dog–human bond through play (the best reward for dogs!), and they're pivotal in honing your pup's interactive social skills. They also improve her essential motor skills (such as paw–eye and paw–mouth coordination) as she learns how to grasp and let go of objects.

Pet stores are full of toys, and friends and family may indulge your doggy with playthings. But he needs only three. With only one or two toys, your pup won't have the accessories he needs to develop coordination, bond with other dogs and humans, and get the right amount of physical and mental stimulation. More than three, and your pup will start to think everything is a toy (think shoes, remote controls, etc.), and the last thing you want is a pup who trashes your stuff.

Choose the size of your pup's toys based on the size of her mouth. Toys should also be strong enough to withstand a dog's powerful jaws and sharp teeth and claws. If you question the durability of a toy, do the "yank test" yourself by starting to pull at it as if it were a wishbone. If it gets to the point where you can see that two adults would be able to rip it apart easily, forget that toy and try another one. (Of course, don't actually rip the toy apart, just get to the point where you can see that the toy would be too fragile for your dog.) Then test the toy for size. If the toy can compress to a size that allows it to go halfway into your pooch's mouth, it's too small and can be a choking hazard. If she can't get her chops around it, the toy is too big. Some toys that you'll find at the pet store are useless; others are downright dangerous. Steer clear of any with plastic eyes or plastic bells and whistles, as these are also potential choking hazards. Simple, minimalist toys are the best; form should follow function.

Once your pup is two and a half months old and has been vaccinated, take another trip to the pet store so she can pick out the toys she prefers. But for now, get just three basic toys (as described below) and have them ready for her before she arrives at your home:

1. a rope/tug toy for playing tug games (you can find strong rope at a hardware store for a tenth of the cost of rope toys at pet stores)

2. a rubber ball or a soft Frisbee for playing fetch

3. something that satisfies your pup's need to chew, suck and be mentally stimulated, such as a Kong toy, a Nylabone or a squeaky toy

Certain human toys are dangerous for dogs:

- Tennis balls are made of material that is so abrasive that it will wear down your pup's teeth like a nail file and cause significant damage.

- Hard plastic Frisbees can damage teeth or bonk your pup in the schnozz.

- Rawhide chew toys get stinky, and since they're designed to splinter and tear, they can easily lodge in your dogs digestive tract.

- Ditto for wood sticks, since bark can also splinter and might contain pesticides.

Puppy Apparel

I'm not suggesting you treat your pup like a doll, but depending on where you live and on your dog's breed (such as small breeds or breeds with short hair), you might have to invest in dog boots and a waterproof coat for the winter. Even if your winters are mild and you have a big, hairy dog, the de-icing salt on sidewalks and roads can burn your puppy's paws. He'll also be tempted to lick his paws clean, and that can make him sick. If you decide against boots or your pup hates wearing them, make sure you rinse his paws thoroughly after an outdoor winter romp. (But don't give up too quickly on the boots! Sometimes it takes a few tries before a dog will tolerate them.) On days when the temperature drops below zero, watch for frostbite on your pup's paws and ears; it will turn his skin bright red before it goes pale. Be aware of your puppy's reaction to the cold and respect that. Just because your pup's birthday suit is a fur coat, it doesn't mean he can endure extreme weather. If you can't tolerate the cold, neither can he.

Puppy Grooming Kit

Grooming is an essential part of taking good care of your pup. And you'll need only a few supplies to keep your four-legged friend clean and healthy:

- a grooming brush with short, firm bristles (though for breeds with longer hair, you may have to invest in a longer-bristled brush as your pup's coat grows)

- a pair of round-tipped scissors for cutting matted hair

- dog shampoo and conditioner (preferably organic)

- a dog toothbrush and toothpaste (preferably organic), but, technically, raw bones and dry kibble will also keep your canine's teeth healthy

Pups and Kids

Be extra mindful of the canine point of view if you have two-legged cuties in your household mix. If you have children in the family, you'll need to do extra prep work, and some dogs will not mix well with little ones. Canines are especially sensitive to toddlers who teeter around, lunging and groping at everything. Because they understand messages by assessing our body language, any awkward movements and an unsteady gait are unnatural to them and could be perceived as either threatening or weak. So any dog could develop unusual behaviour around children.

When considering bringing a puppy into a household where there's already a child, it's important to consider the pooch's size (now and when full grown). It's also essential to assess the age and maturity level of both the dog and the child as well as their individual traits and personalities. Some of my client dogs have developed food- and territory-related aggressions that have unfortunately made them dangerous around kids. Treat-trained dogs who mooch and hover around tables, high chairs, strollers and car seats are especially problematic around kids. Other dogs have guarding instincts that make them overly protective of their little human pack members. Please remember that it's your job to make sure that any dog you introduce into your home has the potential to interact in a healthy way with your kids. You also need to safeguard both species by teaching them the rules of engagement. Here are some tips:

- Before you bring your pup home, start exposing your children to well-behaved mature dogs that you already know. Be sure to teach your kids to be sensitive and respectful toward these dogs as much as possible.

- Teach your children that dogs have highly tuned, sensitive hearing, so they should never yell into or near a dog's ears. Instruct them to avoid using high-pitched tones when communicating with any canines.

- If possible, go to a local dog park and introduce the kids to a few puppies there.

- As soon as your puppy comes home, you must teach both pups and kids the rules of conduct when it comes to letting go of objects . This way everyone will understand that human hands are to be respected. The Tug O' War Game (in Stage 4) is a great way to get started.

- Remember that respect is a two-way street. If we want our puppies and dogs to respect us, every human needs to be respectful of canine bodies and minds.

Cats and Dogs

People who love puppies may also love cats. And they might already have one at home. But if you introduce a puppy to a household already inhabited by a cat, you'll not only have to establish a pack structure with your new canine. You'll also have to teach the puppy that the cat (or cats!) is/are now part of their family pack. Ditto if you are thinking of getting a kitten after you bring a pup home. Dogs and cats don't speak the same "language," so integrating these two species into the same home can be tricky. Cats are all about the physical place and dogs are more concerned with the social aspects. I recommend a little prep work, but if you are consistent and take your time, you will all grow to be one big, happy family! Here are a few scenarios:

Dog Meets Cat
- If you already have a cat and are bringing home a puppy, have a well-behaved dog visit your home a few times before you pick up your pup. Make sure the dog is leashed so you can control the action if one or both species get(s) overexcited.

- When the new puppy arrives, allow the cat some time to sniff and investigate while the pup is still in her crate.

- For the first little while, don't let them interact unless the pup is in her crate or on a leash.

- The puppy and cat shouldn't be left alone together until there's a good level of comfort. That way you can make sure you're always in control of their environment.

- Even after the pets have become used to one another and harmony reigns, make sure the cat always has a safe place to go, where the puppy can't get at him.

- Praise and encourage the puppy when she's gentle and doesn't chase or bark at the cat. And praise the cat when he's gentle around the puppy. Positive reinforcement is vital!

- Keep a canine toy handy so you can distract the puppy if she gets rambunctious around your feline.

Cat Meets Dog
- It would be best not to bring a cat into your home until your pup is house-trained and understands her role in the household pack.

- If possible, have your pup visit adult cats first, so you can figure out how she will react to a feline.

- Look for red flags like chasing or aggressive behaviour. If this kind of activity doesn't go on, give
  the two species time to introduce themselves.

- If your pup shows signs of aggression, please hold
  off on adopting a cat until your pup is three years
  old.

- Before your puppy and new cat (or kitten) meet,
  let the feline explore the puppy's crate. (This is the
  only exception you should make to the "off-limits
  crate" rule.) Then let your pup sniff around so she
  can get used to the smell of the kitten or cat.

- Next, leash up your pup and let her get acquainted
  with the cat under your watchful eyes. Even your
  puppy's most innocent behaviours can trigger a
  vicious reaction from a nervous kitten or cat.

- Don't expect the pets to become best friends right
  away. They'll need to establish their relationship
  at their own pace. And some dogs and cats may
  not become buddies, even though they'll tolerate
  each other.

The Final Countdown:
Setting the Ideal Tone and Vibe

When your pup arrives at your threshold, she will
already have put in eight weeks of living. So it would
be a good idea to get the lowdown on her early weeks
by watching online videos of pups with their canine

moms. And those videos will also give you some of your first lessons in dogspeak. Search "puppies" and "mom" on YouTube first. When the human "directors" remain quiet on set, you'll notice there will be a lot of movement in the canine litter. But there will be very little canine chatter—and virtual silence from the doggy moms while the pups jostle, mouth, play and nurse. There's a spare grace and beauty to these canine interactions.

Now keep on searching YouTube for videos about human parents and babies. Unlike the dog videos, you'll notice a constant stream of high-pitched human chirping and baby talking. Do you see what I'm talking about? How does the baby talk make *you* feel? After watching the quiet interactions of the dogs, I'll bet all that human jabber will really wear on your nerves. Now just imagine how sensitive canine ears would interpret such grating verbal diarrhea? And it's not just *annoying* to canines. They use and interpret high-pitched sounds as signs of distress and pain. So whenever we use this pitch, they view us as weak and hurt, and that is entirely the wrong message an assured dog owner should be sending out.

Now do a search for "cute puppy" plus "baby" videos. Compare the different interactions between pups and human babies. Notice how the puppies cock their ears and appear anxious when they're exposed to high-pitched baby talk? In my books, this would be like being forced to listen to loud, squeaky recordings over and over again. Imagine having to suffer through your life with that kind of babbling? It would drive you batty, right? In my books, it's downright abusive.

Of course, you're going to be excited to have your pup at home, and your tone of voice will reflect that excitement, so even your adult voice may grate on the poor pup's nerves. It's natural to be enthusiastic about a new pet, but just be careful not to get into high-pitched tones around her. Here are some more overarching rules to keep in your back pocket for your first twenty-four hours with your new puppy:

- Constant repetitive talking and commanding confuses dogs and can sometimes make them tune us out. It also desensitizes them, so they'll be less likely to listen to the directions they'll soon be learning—like "Hustle" and "Stop."

- As much as possible, address your pup in a calm tone of voice, using verbal commands sparingly, so each one counts.

- Show your affection for your pup primarily through your actions as a responsible, consistent, assertive and fun-loving caregiver.

My advice and strategies are ultimately about providing as much balance as possible in your pup's life. Keep this concept in mind as you navigate the amazing first year of your pup's life. I don't mean you should strive for constant neutrality: have fun, let the scale tip in a more free-and-easy direction when you're playing, trying new activities and training your pup. Then show more restraint as your pup learns to negotiate the rules and boundaries, as you house-train or when you have to discipline emerging negative behaviours. Always do your part to maintain consistency in all aspects of life with your pup. If you're a well-balanced caregiver, together, you and your pup will be able to scale whatever challenges come along. And you'll reach the ultimate goal: an awesome relationship.

STAGE 3

welcome to the (human) jungle: puppy's first twenty-four hours in your pack

Have you been counting down to this day or what? Your pup is ready for you, and you can't wait to bring him home. It's an exciting time, but please remember that your pup hasn't been looking forward to leaving his digs and moving into yours. In the best of circumstances, he will have been chilling and hanging and playing with his canine pack. And he may have been been gradually exposed to human contact. Of course, you'll be psyched—and if you have kids in the household, they've probably been jacked for weeks—but remember where your pup is coming from: a calm, quiet, warm, nurturing, balanced *canine* pack. You need to do your best to imitate that environment as much as possible. This will reduce your pup's culture shock, and it will also help you capitalize on your pup's natural, instinctual behaviour.

As I said earlier, a pup who has spent at least eight weeks with a well-balanced, healthy canine pack comes to you expecting rules and boundaries. So in Stage 3, I'll be discussing the importance of initiating a playbook of house policies that *you* need to abide by from the start, in order to establish *human* consistency. I've already mentioned some of these things: not letting your pup on the human furniture and not talking in high-pitched tones, for instance. That way you'll create the best possible environment to keep you and your puppy grounded and bonded. If you use these simple techniques consistently, you'll avoid so many potential behavioural issues and other hurdles as your pooch grows up.

The Pickup

Make sure you arrange to pick your puppy up on a Friday or a weekend morning or any other time when you'll have at least forty-eight hours with your pup before the work week begins. Even better, pick her up when you have at least a week's vacation in front of you or when you have the option of taking your pup to work with you, at least for the first few weeks. And don't drive off without your dog crate, collar and leash!

Once the pup is officially yours, the first thing you should do is put on her collar. Put it on over her snout, not from above or behind the ears. Coming in from the ears would make her drop down, and it would then be a lot more difficult to get the collar around her head. Then attach the leash. With sure-footed pooches, walk the pup out to your vehicle and don't pick her up until it's time to put her in.

Here's the correct way to pick up a puppy or any dog, no matter what size:

1. Squat down and slide one hand between the front legs and under the chest area until your hand is palming and supporting the puppy's rib cage and front region.

2. Put your other hand at the top of his hind limbs, just below the tail and butt. This way his back region will be supported and your hand can stabilize both his body and his legs.

3. Never compress your pup's spine. The goal is to keep the body long.

4. As with lifting anything, bend and lift with your knees and keep your back straight.

Once you're in your vehicle, don't put your pup in your lap when you're driving. Put him in the crate. Follow the lifting protocol described above when you get home, placing your pup on the ground (with his leash on) so he can take in the smells, sights and sounds of his new outdoor surroundings for at least a few minutes before you go inside.

Once you're inside, even if you have a large home, you might think you should give your pup a complete house tour. This would actually be too overwhelming for him. For now, just walk your pup around the main living area and as the days pass, slowly introduce him to more rooms. And remember to keep most of the doors closed, especially bathroom doors, laundry room doors and doors to your children's rooms, with all their enticing, but potentially hazardous, stuffed animals and toys. (For a complete list of things to do to puppy-proof your home, see "Things to Watch Out For" at the beginning of Stage 2.)

Stick with the primary living spaces, and resist the temptation to sit down on the couch or any human furniture to cuddle with your pup. Get down on the ground to play. Introduce your pup to his three toys and play with him for a while. If you did end up buying a pup at a pet shop or through a shelter that was unsure about his early history, or if you chose an older pup, he could already be exhibiting behavioural issues like separation anxiety, elimination problems, barking, jumping up and showing rude "table" and social manners. For a dog with these behaviours, you might need to be even more patient and consistent with the strategies and training techniques I'll be discussing throughout this book. Remember the old saying "Rome wasn't built in a day." Ditto for a stellar interspecies bond.

Feeding Time

Your pup might already be hungry or thirsty, so put out some fresh food and water and let him have a meal and a drink. Here are some words to live by when it comes to pups and meal time. (I know I've said some of this stuff before, but it's so important it's worth repeating.)

- Do not feed your pup human food.

- Do not force your pup to sit (or perform any training-related skills) before he eats.

- Some trainers also recommend that you always eat before your dog does. That's often unfair to the pet, though—especially after a long day. I recommend eating before your pup does only if he is seriously trying to gain dominance over you.

- Don't pet, yap at or try to play with your pup while he's eating, and make sure that any children steer clear of getting near his snout. Allow for a decent perimeter of space around his food and water bowls and make that area a human-free zone.

- Refrain from playing and rough-housing with your pup at all times while you're in the kitchen, especially around the stove. Accidents can happen while you're cooking, especially when busy parents have toddlers and a wired pup underfoot. So take the preventive measure of making the kitchen a no-play zone.

- Once your pup has finished eating, store away any extra food for the next meal. I don't recommend allowing your pup to graze on food throughout the day.

- To minimize elimination accidents, don't feed your pup or give him any water after 7 p.m., unless you're a night owl.

House-Training How-To

Within the first hour at home, you should begin house-training your pup by introducing her to her elimination spot. And chances are she might need to pee immediately. Even though lots of young pups rarely show obvious signs that they need to relieve themselves, a dog's body language will often change ever so slightly if she needs to go. She might be playing and suddenly start to squat slightly, so her hind legs splay out behind her. If your young pup starts to squat, she'll probably urinate within seconds, giving you little time to react. That's why I recommend introducing your pup to her elimination zone *before* she starts to squat. As with so many other aspects of puppy training and bonding, the goal is to act preventively so negative behaviours don't happen in the first place. If your pup is more than three months old, she might show more obvious signs of the need for relief, such

> Don't fret if your male pup is squatting to pee. He will typically lift a leg by seven months old, or sometimes even later. It'll happen when your pup is ready.

as heading for a corner, sniffing or digging at the ground, running around in circles, giving you an urgent look or scratching or barking at the door. Regardless of age, pay close attention to every behaviour, movement, gesture and aspect of body language from the start. You'll be surprised how quickly you tap into your pooch's canine behaviours.

The best way to house-train your pup is to teach her how to eliminate outdoors right from the start. If you use newspaper, puppy pads or a litter box, your pup will get used to relieving herself indoors, and it will be a real chore to switch to outdoor training later on. Not only that, but it's quite likely that your puppy won't be able to tell the difference between newspaper, a puppy pad and, say, a blanket, rug or throw pillow. Litter boxes also encourage indoor digging, so a pup might view any potted plant as her own private toilet. Here again, consistency is key. Elimination is one of the primary home-wrecking behaviours that drive my clients to the brink with their mature dogs. So put house-training at the top of your to-do list and do your best to avoid any mixed messages. That way your pup will have a head start on the path to success.

When you come back home after spending hours away from your non-house-trained pup, take her outside to pee and poop before you start playing with her. Some pups will pee when they're excited, and some will even eliminate as soon as they come into contact with a human hand. If your pup is like this, during the initial period, keep her crated while you're out or when you're sleeping. Then, as soon as you return or wake up, take the crate outside and let her out to take care of her business. After that, you can start physically handling and playing with her back in the house. It's also great to play with your pup outdoors, especially if you have a backyard.

Be patient with house-training and try not to get frustrated. Monitor your pup's behaviour as the weeks and months progress, so you can identify the methods she uses to let you know she needs to pee. By the age of three months or so, a pup should be able to hold her bladder for at least eight hours. If she can't, talk to your vet about potential health issues.

Identifying a Puppy Pee-Pee Spot

If you have a backyard, identify one specific spot for elimination. If you live in an apartment, find a patch of grass near the front entrance because you'll probably need to get there quickly when you're half-asleep in the middle of the night. (If you choose a spot farther away, you might regret it—especially in the depths of winter.) Some eight-week-old pups can already hold their bladders for eight hours, but many need to be trained to build up their bladder capacity. And they could be three months old before they get to full capacity. Once your pup is house-trained and can hold his bladder for eight hours or longer, give him plenty of outdoor exercise every morning and evening in a variety of places. If you don't have a backyard, make sure your pup is on her leash when you take her out. A good walk twice a day will satisfy her needs and prevent territorial elimination issues from occurring.

Your Puppy's Pee-Pee Spot

1. Take your leashed pup to the spot you've designated as his "toilet" area.

2. Once you're outside, keep the leash slack and let your pup sniff around as you guide his toward the designated area. Once you're there, stop, and in a calm, neutral voice, say, "Go pee" or "Do your business." (It doesn't really matter what you say as long as the specific message is simple and consistent.)

3. Chances are your pup will urinate first. When he's finished, say, "Good pee" in a calm but upbeat voice. Then let him sniff around for a few minutes. He might then defecate. If he does, say, "Good poop." (You could also say, "Good job" or "Nice one" or whatever you want to say, but remember to keep it simple and encouraging. And say it only once so it doesn't lose its potency.)

4. Follow up the verbal praise with a good chest scrunch (described later in this chapter).

5. After your pup has relieved himself, take note of the time. It's important to keep track of his initial bladder-capacity threshold and also to note how it changes. Write the bladder-holding time down on a piece of paper or in a notebook and call it your pup's "Elimination Diary." Keep it in a handy place, so you can easily record later times.

Some young pups can hold their bladders for hours from the start (and even through the night), while others take weeks or months to build up bladder endurance.

6. The next time your pup eliminates, follow the method outlined above once again and note the time. Wait the same amount of time plus an additional fifteen minutes before you take him out again.

7. If your pup doesn't go right away, don't rush the process. If you're stressed, your pup will pick up on it, and we all know that when we're stressed, we aren't in the ideal mood for relieving ourselves. You want to make the event as pleasant as possible. Don't shout at your pup or get agitated. If your pup doesn't go within ten minutes, go back inside and try again in another fifteen minutes.

8. Was your pup able to hold his bladder for those additional fifteen minutes? If not, see the next section on elimination accidents. If your pup was successful, add another fifteen-minute period to your timer.

9. Take your pup out for relief just before you go to bed. But note that he might still have to go during the night, especially if he had a late meal and drink. I highly recommend that you keep your pup's bed or crate in your bedroom (and if crated, keep the door

open to prevent crate accidents). That way you can respond promptly and get your pup outside when he needs to go. During these late-night outings, skip the leashing and walking part if you have a backyard "potty." Instead, pick your pup up to shorten the trip. Or take the entire crate outside and open the crate door once you're at the elimination zone.

Dealing With Elimination Accidents

Expect accidents, especially during the first few days and weeks. That's one of the main reasons I recommend taking at least a long weekend off work during the initial house-training phase—or cashing in on some vacation time or taking your pup to work. If these aren't options, consider hiring a pet sitter to come by your home at least once in the middle of your work day to help with the house-training and play with your pup for a while. Walk your sitter through the protocol described under "Your Pup's Pee-Pee Spot" and ask him to please be respectful of your set rules of conduct, including refraining from high-pitched baby talk and cuddling the dog on human furniture.

If you discover your pup has had an accident while you were in another room or when you were out, don't have a meltdown or blow your cool. The goal is to remain calm and in control. If *you* have a tantrum every time your pup steps out of line, your pup will tune in to *your* bad behaviour and potentially see it as an opportunity to act out and engage in negative attention-seeking behaviours.

Here's what you should do if your puppy has an elimination accident:

1. Walk him back to the "spill zone" and say in a firm voice, "Unacceptable" or simply "No." (Again, the exact word or phrase doesn't matter; it's the firm tone of voice that counts.) Clean and disinfect the spill zone immediately to remove any trace of the scent, and while you're doing that, ignore your pup. Don't talk or make any eye contact.

2. If your pup tries to get you to play or if he starts whimpering, say, "Leave it" or simply "No" in a firm tone. Then ignore him for fifteen minutes. Don't storm out of the room in a huff. Stay within sight range so you can make sure he's not acting out, but keep busy doing your own thing.

Territorial Elimination Issues

If you're house-training an older pup, during walks she might try to pull over every few steps to pee. Wild dogs urinate to mark territory, and your pup might come to you doing the same thing. This can happen when a previous owner took her on the same stroll around the same block twice a day—neglecting her need to explore new terrain all the time. So your puppy would have become bored with the routine and now considers any route she takes as her own private sanctuary. As a result, she compulsively marks every bush, pole and flowerbed. And when confronted with the smell of another dog's urine or feces, she'll feel compelled to cover that scent with her own. I see a lot of city dogs stuck in this routine because they're exposed to the same mundane walk every day. While you shouldn't encourage or allow any forms of territorial behaviour, you'll understand your pup better if you realize that she acts this way instinctually because her doggy needs haven't been met and she's been poorly trained.

> ### Save That "Stop" Word!
>
> Don't use the word "Stop" in response to any misbehaviours. That's a word you'll want to save for teaching basic and advanced training, to street-proof your pet against hazards like traffic. If you use it for other things, your pup will become desensitized to its power.

If your pup comes to you doing this, it's your job to curb the behaviour. It takes about twenty seconds for a pup to empty his bladder, so if he's tinkling for a few seconds every few steps, stop walking and tell your pup to pee. Don't let him pull on the leash and seek out new turf. Wait in your spot for a minute, and if he doesn't continue to pee on that spot, start walking briskly and don't allow him to stop and mark for at least a few minutes. (The key is that you control the movement. That way your pup will get the crystal-clear message that you are in charge of the pace and the terrain.) Stop again and tell your pup to pee. Repeat this process every time your pup starts to tinkle—until he stops the behaviour. But make sure you do more than just correct his acquired habit. Give him the fun and adventure of being exposed to a variety of different environments, including different walks in your neighbourhood. This will meet your pup's needs and also help stop him from peeing and pooping to mark territory.

One of my dog buddies, Rudy (a schnoodle), is a mature, balanced and well-trained canine, so he rarely pulls on the leash. But when he does, I know he means, "Dude, I've been inside too long, and now I need to do my business. Pick up the pace. I'm bee-lining for that fire hydrant." In other words, he's pulling on the leash to remind me that his canine needs must be respected. Any mature, well-behaved dog will use this method. Make sure you don't punish your pup or dog for pulling on the leash in situations like this. When a well-trained dog pulls on the leash every so often (and when you haven't been meeting a legitimate need), he's doing nothing wrong. In fact, when this happens, you should reward your pup for expressing his needs in a healthy way.

The Paw-Grappling Game

My philosophy is to always balance out any type of training with loads of fun playtime. Of course, pups are always dialed up for play, but if *you* initiate and engage in playing with your pup, your pup will be dialed into *you*. And that's the ideal way to stimulate a bond. Once your pup is tuned into you and into

CUTE = CAREFUL

Psychologists did a test to find out whether humans become more cautious as a result of being around cute little creatures. They exposed people to images of puppies and kittens and then to pictures of dogs and cats.[8] To gauge behaviour, after the subjects viewed each set of images, their dexterity levels were tested while they played the kids' game Operation.

The researchers found that people showed "superior performance" after viewing the pups and kitties and theorized that "human sensitivity to those possessing cute features may be an adaptation that facilitates caring for delicate human young." In my opinion, this kind of sensitivity can be really beneficial when people are dealing with young pups. But trust me, they'll start manipulating us with their cutes if we treat them like infants. Remember, your pup is a canine, not a human baby!

paying attention when you play with her, take the opportunity to sneak in a few *educational* games.

Pups are ready-made to frolic and romp around, but when they're very young and fragile, people seem to think they have to treat them with kid gloves by babying them, cradling them and smothering them with hugs. Humans are especially prone to this reaction when they have a small-breed pup. While I think pups are much more rare and precious than any *objet d'art*, they do have to be treated like canines! And the Paw Grappling Game is ideal for playing and bonding with teeny, tiny pups. It'll keep their minds active and build up their physical aptitude and paw–eye coordination. Here's how to play:

1. Get down on all fours with your pup.

2. Curb your talking. Ideally, say nothing at all, so you can really tap into the power of body language and movement.

3. Use your index finger like a hand to grapple, wrestle with and play with your small pup.

4. For larger-breed pups with more power and weight, add more fingers to the mix.

5. Use your index finger to nudge and "paw" at your pup's body.

6. If your pup bites you at any point, say, "Ouch" in a high-pitched voice. (Chances are the sound will startle your pup into releasing your finger from his little teeth.)

7. Tap your index finger on top of his front paws to intensify the game. Your pup will probably respond by one-upping you, putting his paw over your index finger. That's excellent!

8. Now take your index finger out from under his paw. Then one-up him again by tapping his fuzzy little paw-top with your index finger.

9. Continue the paw–finger game for a while, but wrap it up by scoring the last "win"—that last one-up with your finger over his paw.

As the weeks progress and your pup grows and becomes stronger, add additional fingers to the mix while you're playing and wrestling. Your pup will also continue to "grow into his limbs" and build up dexterity and motility. That is, his body will grow more in proportion to his gangly legs, and he'll be able to handle objects and move with greater skill. When this happens, notch up the level of strength you bring into playing and wrestling with him.

The Chest Scrunch and the Importance of Physical Bonding

I'm a firm believer in rewarding dogs with physical forms of praise, but most people limit their affection by praising their puppy or dog with a pat on the top of the head. Instead, I recommend praising your pup with a good chest scrunch, focusing on an area of your pup's body that has a lot of muscle and deep tissue. Dogs love it, and the technique is simple, whether your pup is standing, sitting or lying down.

1. Using your fingertips, start massaging your pup's chest area, in the muscles between the front legs.

2. Do the chest massage for a few seconds if you're rewarding basic training wins like house-training and the sit-stay training I'll discuss in Stage 5.

3. Start with minimal pressure and then increase the pressure, depending on the age and size of your pup.

Step-by-Step Full Body Massage

I also recommend daily doggy massages. It makes your pup feel great, especially after a long, strenuous romp, and it helps you get to know your pup's body, so you'll be able to spot any lumps, cuts or rashes she might have later. It also teaches your pup to be very comfortable when vets or strangers touch her. Of course, I hope your pup will never be injured, but if she is, that trip to the vet or dog hospital will be so much less painful and scary for her if she trusts the hands and intentions of humans.

On this first day together, giving your new pup a massage is also one of the best ways to bond with her, and it's an ideal method for helping her relax before you turn in for the night. Spend at least fifteen minutes a day massaging her. But don't try to massage your pup when she's wired for sound and would prefer to play. Ditto if she's already sleeping. The last thing you want to do is have her associate human touch with anything unpleasant or annoying.

1. Keep the talk to a minimum and always use a neutral, calm, subdued voice as you massage your pup's body.

2. If you have kids, let them watch the first few times, so they understand that the pup

should be touched gently and soothingly. Once they understand that, they can start massaging her as well.

3. Use your fingertips and start by applying gentle pressure, as if you were checking an avocado for ripeness. You can increase the pressure as the days pass and your pup grows stronger and becomes accustomed to your touch.

4. If at any time during a massage your pup yelps or whines in a high-pitched tone, it means, "Ouch!" Immediately stop touching your pup. By releasing your hold, you're responding with an "I'm sorry, buddy." Don't gush with a bunch of high-pitched apologies. In the canine world, actions almost always speak louder than words.

5. Move on to other body parts, but then return to the hotspot (where your pup felt hurt) and try again, using less pressure. If your pup continues to react with an ouch every time you touch that spot over the next few days, consult your vet.

After a few weeks of massaging your pup daily, start introducing him to a new set of human hands while you're watching over the action. In Stage 4 I'll recommend letting your pup get to know a few humans and well-behaved, vaccinated adult dogs, so recruit one of your pet's new human buds to do a

M · M · M · MASSAGING

D oing a massage is a great way to get to know every square inch of your pup. While you're massaging, listen to the way your pup breathes. Note that the spine is cooler than the stomach region. Pay attention to the paws, looking for any debris that might be wedged around the paw pads. Check the ears for ticks and bugs or any rank smells. If you discover any of these, consult your vet. Check your pup's eyes for unusual things like black spots or yellow or bloodshot eyeballs. Some breeds need to have their eyes cleaned weekly and some have excess mucus that crusts up. Clean this gunk out of your pup's eyes regularly. First, place a warm washcloth over the eye to soften the crust. Then wipe the gunk off gently.

puppy massage. Do this approximately twice weekly for the next few months. It will help boost your pup's confidence and also help him learn to trust others and especially you, knowing that you've literally got his back.

Mouth Massage

The mouth massage is a great way to check the health of your pup's teeth. It also lays the ground-work for you to establish a clear rule: that she has to be gentle and careful whenever a human finger or hand makes contact with her mouth and teeth.

Start by asking for permission by tugging very gently at your pup's jowls (the skin over her jaws), near her mouth. Then, using your index finger, start rubbing her gums and teeth, especially the back teeth, where plaque builds up the most. Check your pup's breath. It doesn't have to be the sweetest-smelling breath in the world, but if it really stinks, she might have an abscessed tooth or a serious internal illness. If you decide to do daily tooth brushing, I recommend not introducing the toothbrush until your third day with your pup. Then add the toothpaste on the fourth day. You don't want to overwhelm her with too much stimulation. Ditto with bathing right away. We'll get to that in Stage 4.

Your Pup's First Night

Young puppies spend the majority of their time sleeping, so make sure you don't overwhelm your pup with too much activity on his first day with you. When the time comes for you to go to bed, take your pup out for a pee break and then lead him to his nighttime bed. As I mentioned earlier, it's a great idea to crate or bed your pup in your room, especially during the first few months. But please don't cave in to the temptation to let your pup sleep with you in your bed — or with any humans for that matter. That said, it's not good to isolate your pup by making him sleep in an area too far from all human activity. For an eight-week-old pup who's spent his entire life snuggling with his siblings and mom, sudden isolation could give him quite the culture shock. So try to bed your pup within hearing range, if not sight range.

Teaching "Bed"

1.   Lead your pup to her bed or crate. Bring
     along a toy that your pup can chew or suck.

2.   If her bed is upstairs, she might not be able
     to make it on her own. In that case it's okay
     to pick your pet up. Otherwise, never pick
     up your pup to take her anywhere. That will
     teach learned helplessness, which you want
     to avoid at all costs. Besides, most pups eight
     weeks old or older will be able to get up the
     stairs without any problem.

3.   Once you get to the pup's bed, place the toy
     on it, point to it and say, "Your bed" with a
     bit of enthusiasm. Again, your specific words
     don't matter as long as they're simple and
     clearly enunciated.

4.   Next, say, "Go to bed" in a firm, calm voice
     and point again. I recommend pointing be-
     cause dogs learn to respond well to pointing
     gestures, whether you're teaching them
     something or playing.

5.   Don't pick up your pup and place her on
     the bed or inside the crate. Let her get to
     bed on her own steam so she doesn't feel
     forced. If she feels forced, she'll associate
     bedtime with something unpleasant.

6. Once your pup is on her bed or in her crate, give her a brief chest scrunch and say, "Good girl" or give her some other encouraging words.

7. If your pup gets out of bed, repeat the above directives until she starts to understand and appreciate that this space is entirely hers and is meant for chilling and sleeping.

Remember, your duty is to control all the action not because you're a tyrant, but to relieve your dog from the burden of thinking *she has to be* in the driver's seat 24/7. Whatever the age of your canine, she didn't read an operator's manual before she came into your life. So it's up to you to teach your pup rules and boundaries. Teaching "Go to bed" or "Time to chill" will come in handy throughout your dog's life whenever you need your dog to relax, no matter what time of day. But remember, never use your dog's bed as a timeout zone when you're disciplining bad attitude.

Dealing With Late-Night Whimpering

Your pup might whine in the middle of the night if he needs to pee or poop. But if he starts whimpering as soon as your head hits the pillow, you'll know he's just feeling anxious. It might not seem like a big deal if you rush over to comfort your pup or talk baby talk to him, cooing and cawing, during his first few days with you, but it is! If you do that, you'll be teaching your dog to be helpless and feel insecure. You'll teach your pup that you'll reward these negative behaviours with attention. I've met many dogs who've developed serious separation anxiety because they weren't taught to be comfortable on their own. I've also met plenty of pups who parrot insecurity as a form of manipulation. They have their two-legged owners wrapped around their paws before they've reached four months of age. Don't set your relationship up for these issues.

Instead, let your pup whimper for a few seconds, but if it continues, use a firm voice and say, "No noise." This phrase will also come in handy whenever your pup or dog barks excessively. (Read about initial and advanced patience training in Stages 4 and 7 for more details and some insights into why dogs bark too much.) In many cases dog owners are at least partly to blame for excessive barking because *they* bark and holler repeatedly and excessively at their pups. Whether or not you've ended up doing this, if your pup continues to whimper, say, "No noise" again, but put a bit more force into your voice. (As I said earlier, never use the phrase "Stop it." The word "Stop" should be reserved for training.)

STAGE 4

puppy imprinting: umbilical training, chew training and grooming

Did you get much sleep during your first night with the pup? Perhaps not. This is another reason why I hope you booked a few days off work before bringing your pet home!

Whether you got enough sleep or not, once you both wake up, it will be time to start training your pooch, setting and maintaining more rules and boundaries and also providing daily walks and mental stimulation. Between the age of eight and eleven weeks, puppies sleep a lot, but once they're awake, watch out! They'll be playing nonstop and bouncing around you. This can be fun at first, but if you're trying to relax or do chores around the house, it can become an unwelcome distraction. To nip this problem in the bud, I've developed something called "umbilical training," which will show your pup that you're the leader of the pack without making his life miserable. At about eleven weeks of age, your pup will start to follow you around, so it's crucial, right from the early days, to build up his trust in your leadership and your ability to be a dependable caregiver. And umbilical training is a great way to do this. It's also a wonderful way to bond with your pup.

So now I'll walk you through the umbilical training method and give you tips on how to tweak it for your canine's size, dexterity and maturity level.

Umbilical: The Lifeline

I call this type of training "umbilical" because it literally and figuratively connects you with your pup and harnesses your pup's primary method of canine communication: physical movement and body language. Think about it: dogs like to be on the move, taking in the smells, sights and sounds. There's a simple, spare and elegant beauty to the movements of a dog pack, but this smooth operation depends on each member of the pack being highly sensitive to the others' body language. And movement is a top priority as the pack searches for food and shelter. Movement and physical gestures are also vital elements when it comes to teaching young pups rules, boundaries and discipline—and for correcting negative behaviours when a canine breaks the rules.

Umbilical is simple. Instead of walking your dog with the leash in hand, you attach the leash around your waist, like a belt, so your hands are free and you can walk, stride and run naturally and assertively. This sends a crystal-clear message to your puppy that you're the leader, in control of all movement. It allows your pup to tap into your personal rhythm and to learn your mannerisms. Umbilical is also the most effective way to dial into your pup's body language and into his instinctual need for movement. It's the best way to establish and maintain a bond and teach your pup that you're an assertive pack leader, leading and caring for him. Simply put, it says, "I've got your back, little bud. I'm your leader." It's also a super-cool, hands-free method of training that doesn't even seem like training because you can do it anytime: while you're at home chilling, doing errands, sitting at the computer or watching a movie. On umbilical, your pup is paying attention to you no matter what you're doing, and a pup who pays attention to you is a pup who is fully engaged. Since you're literally connected to him, umbilical also provides a great opportunity to keep watch over your pup's behaviours, allowing you to interrupt any negative behaviours so they don't become bad habits. This is especially helpful when it comes to house-training and chew training.

Umbilical has another bonus: it harnesses the strongest region of *your* body, your core, so you don't have to strain your wrists and shoulders. You might not feel any strain when your pup is a featherweight, but your shoulders will start to bark once your pup is taking the lead at four months of age, especially if she's of a large breed.

It's ideal to do umbilical training daily for the first two weeks you have your pup. After that initial period, I recommend doing umbilical at least three times per week for the rest of your pet's puppy life. This is especially important during the terrible twos (when your pup is seven to nine months old) and after you've been separated from your pup for longer than a few days.

Keep your pup's canine rules of conduct in mind as you do umbilical. Remember that even tiny movements say a whole lot in dogspeak. Think about the way dog parents express themselves. A mother rarely ever barks or growls at her pups. If the mom is feeding her pups and she wants to get up, she doesn't physically move each puppy away; she just gets up and moves. Her puppies learn to understand her movements and power. They don't have the capability to get out of mom's way at first, but during the first six weeks of their lives, they'll certainly learn how to do that!

Similarly, when a canine mom educates, interrupts or corrects unwanted behaviours, she speaks primarily through her motions and actions—by dropping her nose down to nudge the pups or by picking them up by the scruffs of their necks and placing them somewhere else. She's not hurting her puppies when she does this, but with each movement, she underlines the fact that she's in control. Out in nature, a hawk or eagle or some other predator could scoop up her pups. So mom knows her pups must learn the rules of conduct within the canine pack. Otherwise, they would risk being cast out or, worse, maimed or killed in a dog fight or eaten by a predator. Her discipline is about maintaining the pup's safety and well-being. It's a beautiful act.

The most serious canine correction I've witnessed was carried out by a Doberman mom who was teaching two wired little pups not to venture beyond a certain distance. They were living in a clean pen in a barn on a farm. She barked to warn the dogs it wasn't acceptable to move beyond the "safe" zone, but when they broke the rule, she gently picked up each pup by the scruff of the neck and brought them back to the pen. Both puppies once again ventured beyond the boundary, at which point the mom snapped into action with a serious discipline. She swiftly picked up one pup, brought it back into the pen and threw it against the barn wall. Then she did the same with the second pup and promptly walked away from them. Those puppies' feelings might have been hurt, but they weren't physically harmed. They certainly got the message that they had broken a rule and that when the rule was broken twice, there were undesirable consequences.

A canine mom doesn't discipline just because she has nothing better to do. There's always a lesson involved and a basic set of actions meant to send a definite message: if a pup does anything disadvantageous to himself or to the canine pack, he is accountable for those actions.

Of course, I'm not recommending that you use physical force to teach your pup the rules of the human pack, but it's important to respect your pup's point of view, take into account what he will respond to and translate that into something that works for both of you. If you ask me, umbilical is simply the most positive type of training in existence. It's the ideal method for dialing into dogspeak and harnessing your pup's innate abilities while at the same time teaching him to respect you as the pack leader.

The amount of time you spend daily on umbilical with your pup will depend on the age, size and physical maturity of your pup. If you have a tiny, eight-week-old stumblebum of a critter, limit your umbilical sessions to brief ten-minute sessions, move at a slow pace and spend the majority of your umbilical time relaxing. The chief goal is to bond with your pup, and young pups need a lot of sleep, so never force your pup to move around a lot when she's tired. Start an umbilical session when your pup is in an energetic and playful mood. Respect the fact that pups need to build up their fortitude and confidence by spending some time alone daily too.

If you're relaxing and your pup is too, you can do umbilical for longer periods of time. If you have a small-breed puppy with stubby legs who's still really clumsy and has yet to develop good motility, you'll need to be gentle and respectful of her fragile physique. Be careful not to make her do so much during

No Leash, Thank You!

Rudy, a dog owned by one of my clients, heavily resisted being walked on a leash. If your young pup is like that, see the "Leash Standoffs" section later in this chapter for some advice on how to deal with that problem. I know from experience that initial umbilical is sometimes impossible. If this is the case, put it on the back burner for a few weeks and, instead, do the Eat the Leash Exercise described right after "Leash Standoffs" later in this chapter.

the first weeks and months that she can't keep up with you. For larger-breed pups who are already bounding around, I'd recommend introducing more intensive umbilical right away and doing it for two straight weeks, two hours a day, in six nonconsecutive twenty-minute periods.

Step-by-Step Umbilical
Here's my step-by-step umbilical training guide:

1. Thread the clip end of a six-foot leash through the handle at the other end so the leash becomes a circular loop that will serve as a sort of waist belt for you.

2. Step into the loop and pull the leash circle up until it fits comfortably around your waist. (Never begin umbilical by putting the leash circle over your head like a sweater. This is not safe! Get into the habit of doing it feet first.)

3. Attach the leash clip to your pup's Martingale collar and double-check that the collar is properly fitted. When the leash is taut and triangulated, the two collar rings should be one thumbnail length apart.

4. Allow for some slack on the leash when you're standing beside your pup. If you're very tall and/or your pup is a small breed, loop the leash through your belt loop instead of putting it around your waist.

5. Go about your business. Start by moving around your home or take your pup outside for a walk.

And that's umbilical. Simple but effective. It's the best way for you and your puppy to get to know each other and tap into each other's instinctual movements. Is your pup paying attention to you? Looking up at you as if to say, "Wow, okay, this is interesting! What's next?" That's the ideal goal: to have your pup dialed in and attentive. Wrap up each session with some playtime to reward your pup for good behaviour. Unleash your pup and have a play romp, play with one of his toys, do a game of tug or go for a walk.

Here are a few things to keep in mind while you're practising umbilical:

- Don't touch the leash. Pretend it's not there.

- Move with confidence—with your shoulders back, chin up and chest out.

- If your pup gets ahead of you or underfoot, or if the leash strains at all, turn and change directions so you're always in the lead.

- If your pup continues to get in your path, don't move *around* your pup. Instead, keep changing directions.

- Don't step on your puppy's toes, but don't step around them either. If your pup gets underfoot,

GROWING UP UMBILICAL

Puppies younger than eleven weeks will likely be shadowing you all the time, so if the leash strains or your pup gets underfoot during umbilical it's because he's probably still a bit unstable on his feet. In that case change directions every time your pup gets in your way, but don't act like a yo-yo, and resist jerking your pup around.

If your pup is eleven to fifteen weeks old, he'll likely start walking by your side, so he'll rarely get in your way. But at this age, a pup can already read your movements, and if you're too slow, your body language won't be adequate enough for dogspeak.

At fifteen weeks, pups start taking the lead. Now you'll have to increase your speed and change directions more quickly to maintain your position as pack leader.

keep moving in the same direction, but adjust your stride so you can put your foot down just shy of his toes.

- Gauge your movements based on your pup's athletic ability as he grows and becomes more coordinated.

- Be considerate of size with small-breed pups, but keep your movement as fluid as possible. Before long, you'll learn to move assertively while on umbilical, without hesitation.

- With larger-breed puppies, allow your leg to make contact with your dog's body and allow yourself to exert slight pressure on his body to get him to move out of the way. Remember, you're not meant to be a bowling ball, but you're also not meant to be a butterfly. Don't step around your pup. Keep your lines of movement straight.

The goal is to dictate any and all movement so that your pup is following your lead, especially as you go through doorways or up and down stairs or when you're responding to anything like a phone call or a knock on the door. Implement umbilical whenever you can fit it into your busy schedule. One of the great things about it is that you can do umbilical even while you're doing laundry and household chores, while you're sitting at the computer, when you're relaxing and, for mobile pups, when you're running errands outside.

During the first week of training, make sure that at least half of the time you're on umbilical, you're either relaxing while your pup sits or lies on the ground beside you or you're doing fun things (like playing tug on the ground or in the backyard). Umbilical should be a pleasant activity with the primary goal of establishing and maintaining a literal and figurative bond between you and your pup.

As your umbilical training progresses, continue to change your movements slightly, to match your pup's increasing physical abilities. It might take days or weeks for your pup to build up physical prowess, so be understanding and work *with* your pup's skills, not against them.

Umbilical Training With Kids

I think it's wise to involve your kids in all aspects of puppy training, taking into account the age, size and maturity level of both species, but it's important for all members of the household pack to work from the same playbook. So before you start, be sure to teach your kids the rules of conduct and how they relate to your pup's unique canine view of the world. Don't forget to stress that all humans (even tiny ones!) are the pack leaders and the puppy needs to yield to their authority. Explain to your kids that they must be the boss at all times. They'll probably take to that philosophy lickety-split, but make sure they're not rude and obnoxious with their leadership powers. If you feel more comfortable, do umbilical and play tug games (as rewards) with your pup yourself for the first few weeks. After that, you can start to allow supervised dog–child play.

Of course, each individual puppy and dog is unique, but your puppy's fragile stage won't last long, so it's great for younger kids to be involved during this early developmental period. This is especially true for large-breed dogs who will outweigh them within weeks. Acclimatize the kids to the basics first, such as no pups on furniture, no interacting with the puppy while your kids are eating or sleeping, no overcoddling, no playing kissy face and especially no trapping the pup with long hugs that will only irritate and upset her.

Teach the kids how to participate in basic caregiving activities, like picking up poop and giving gentle puppy massages under your supervision. Start hands-on training by having your children shadow you as you do indoor and outdoor umbilical. Use every opportunity to teach your kids to be assertive and consistent with their movements, tone of voice and general interactions with the puppy. Then, as they get the hang of the basic rules and the tone they should use, start allowing your children to hold the leash during walks while you stay close, ready to take over again if the dog starts taking too much control. As a rule of thumb, kids who respond best to umbilical are typically around eight or nine years old because they are more in tune with the concept of responsibility. But that's not to say that your six-year-old shouldn't participate if she's keen and able. Usually, the novelty wears off pretty quickly, though, so hold your kids accountable for their caregiving and training responsibilities.

KIDS AND UMBILICAL

When are children ready to take on umbilical? To some extent, that's a personal choice. My niece Mia was four when she started working with Jack, the German shepherd, and she started umbilical at about six years of age with Jackson, her miniature golden doodle. But I knew those dogs and had already determined that they were well behaved and had no aggressive tendencies. Gauge your comfort level based on the size and traits of your pup, and don't ever let kids do umbilical unsupervised. A small child should not work with a bulldozer Rotti or any dog with behavioural issues until those issues have been curbed successfully.

Safeguarding Kids

At first, you should expect that your puppy will try to get underfoot when your children are around her or she'll try to yank your kids around a little bit when they have her on the leash. Until your pooch has had proper umbilical training and has learned to understand that humans are the pack leaders, she could innocently harm a child. So be aware and vigilant whenever little people are around. Here are a few doggy behaviours that you should be wary of during any canine–child interaction. They don't necessarily indicate aggressiveness, but they shouldn't be tolerated around children and should be corrected as soon as possible.

Re-evaluate any child–puppy contact if your puppy does any of these things:

1. nips at your child's pants or feet or jumps up at your child during walks, umbilical training or at any other time

2. tucks her tail between her legs when kids are around (this may indicate fear or insecurity, which can result in aggressive behaviour)

3. bares her teeth or growls deeply (not a play growl) when interacting with little ones (this could indicate that your pup or dog is sending a "Get away from me" warning sign, which if unheeded, could result in aggression)

PUPPY–CHILD EMPATHY

Behaviour researchers often point out that early exposure to dogs is great for teaching kids empathy. A recent study from Japan has also underlined the importance of child–canine bonding.[9] The experiment compared dogs that had rarely socialized with kids with pooches that had had contact with preschool children during the critical early socialization period (when the pups were three to twelve weeks old). The researchers found that dogs who had been exposed to kids as young pups exhibited no aggressive or excited behaviour when, as grown dogs, they were exposed to a volunteer child. They also didn't have significantly increased heart rates (which could indicate fear or aggression). By comparison, the rarely socialized dogs exhibited aggressive behaviour even when the volunteer child in the study simply entered the room and called the dog's name.

4. exhibits any other potentially negative body language, especially when your pup or dog seems to stand at attention, with body squared off, head raised and neck extended (With some breeds, the hair on the neck and back stands up. This is called raising the hackles, and it could indicate anger or fear. In soft-haired or curly-haired pups, the hackles won't be obvious, so this is another reason why pups need to be watched carefully when they're around kids.)

Leash Standoffs

You might have a puppy who came into your life with incredible tenacity and defiance, and he might not take to being collared and leashed. Every time you try to take him for a walk, he might put on the brakes and refuse to move. My client-dog Rudy was like that when he came to his owner Daniela at seven weeks of age. That little featherweight refused to budge as soon as Daniela tried to walk him. Of course, this kind of behaviour makes outdoor elimination training very difficult, and it sure causes a lot of friction during walks.

If you have a pup like this, put the umbilical training on hold. Get your pup used to wearing his collar for the first four days. Then, on the fifth day, attach the leash but don't hold it. Let it drag on the ground for anywhere from a few days up to a week. If your puppy is still really young and you're house-training and have to get your pup from place to place, pick him up by the scruff of the neck, the way a canine mom does. Some small-breed pups can be scruffed for many months or even years, but to err on the side of caution, I recommend that you stop scruffing a pup when he's about eleven weeks old.

By Week 2, start holding the leash and leading your pup for ten-minute walk sessions. If your puppy is resistant and holds his ground, refusing to budge, you've got a stand-off on your hands. My Eat the Leash Exercise is designed to curb this sort of behaviour, but remember to practise any and all initial leash control on soft surfaces like carpet, grass or slick laminate hardwood. (This will prevent abrasions on your pup's sensitive paws.) Start a session after you've done a little playing with your pup to burn off some energy, but never do training when your pup is already really tired and needs to sleep. I've seen these standoffs last for many minutes—even up to fifteen minutes—before the pup becomes tired and succumbs to his owner's control.

Eat the Leash Exercise

1. Attach the leash to your pup and kneel down, facing her, with your shoulders and hips square to hers. You should be separated by the length of the leash, and the leash should be slightly slack.

2. Hold on to the handle of the leash with one hand, so your thumb and index finger are gripping the leash.

3. Now, with the thumb and index finger of your other hand, start "eating" the leash, one finger length at a time. That is, pull the leash toward you, one finger length at a time. Each time you pull with one hand, let the hand that's holding the leash handle grab the part of the leash that you've now pulled toward you.

4. Eating the leash is like pulling a boat toward a dock by gradually pulling in more and more of the line (the rope) attached to the boat. You would do that with both of your hands, one hand at a time.

5. Continue eating the leash gradually and increasing the tension. Your pup might start to give in to that tension and move toward you. If not, you're at an impasse. Your pup will need to give in, but very tenacious pups will try to make you cave instead. Don't let that happen!

6. Once your pup does budge, don't praise her. Congratulate your puppy only when she moves freely with you, not while she's exhibiting dominant behaviour and caving only because she's tired of fighting the leash.

7. Do this exercise four times a day for a week, and if your pup continues challenging your control of the leash, increase the number of sessions to a maximum of eight sessions daily. Keep doing the exercises until your pup understands the message that you're in control of all movement while she's on-leash.

8. While your pup must eventually surrender control, make sure you don't drag her along behind you at any point. The pads of a young pup's paws are extra sensitive, and you don't want those pads to bleed. Be persistent in acclimatizing your tenacious pup to the leash and don't give up. You'll eventually see progress.

Remember that young pups need to earn respect in order to eventually become street-safe on-leash.

Only then is it possible to start off-leash training. Rudy, the featherweight pup, was off-leash trained by the age of seven months. But he had to earn that liberty by gradually habituating to human leadership. View a tenacious pup not as a disadvantaged or weak little fluff ball but instead as a persistent and daring individual. Harness those traits to both you and your pup's advantage because they'll come in very handy as your relationship evolves and you face new training and bonding challenges together. Don't be impatient; be equally persistent.

The Facts of Puppy Life: Chewing, Teething, Nipping and Mouthing

Has your pup already taken a bite out of your shoes? started eating your leather couch? sucked the varnish right off your hardwood door frames? Puppies are curious at this age, and they will chew and destroy any reachable human possessions because of their innate curiosity and their need to explore their new environment with their paws, mouths and investigative minds. Your pup sees himself as a fact finder on a mission to identify anything and everything that has an interesting smell, taste or texture. Remember that at this early stage, these behaviours are natural and the damage is happening accidentally. That's why consistent house-training and chew training are imperative.,

Young pups, like babies, also go through a teething phase and need to have toys that curb the discomfort of having new teeth push through their gums. And, of course, the toys will also help satisfy the canine urge to chew things over. Pups are clueless about the rules of conduct in the human world and need to be thrown a bone in the form of guidance. Otherwise, they'll treat your possessions as their own. Ditto for a puppy whose previous owners neglected to meet his canine need for constant physical exercise in a variety of new and different locations. And ditto (on an even larger scale) for a dog who has had the misfortune of being treat-trained so he feels entitled to all those so-called goodies (which I consider to be a nasty bag of cheap and dangerous tricks). I've met so many treat-trained dogs who go ape over these dried-up morsels that they view anything standing between their mouths and those treats as public enemy number one. I've said it before and I'll say it again: treat training is a recipe for disaster. Don't do it.

Although I strongly believe that some breed characteristics aren't set in stone, it's important to take them into account when it comes to behavioural issues. For example, we want the Jack Russell terrier to chase balls, and we love it if she catches the mouse in the attic. We laugh when the Border collie herds or corrals the kids playing street hockey. But as soon as that terrier goes chasing after a squirrel at the park or the collie nips someone, we don't think it's so funny. These behaviours don't typically take root until about nine months of age, after a pup's personality emerges, so with a little luck, you won't have to tackle them from the get-go. The key is to be aware of your puppy's needs and keep in mind that when we tolerate certain canine behaviours when it suits *us*, our domestic dogs become confused and sometimes downright hostile. Because they don't know how to act, we often leave them with no choice but to *act out* by engaging in negative behaviours. That's why it's so important to maintain consistent house rules, to satisfy our dogs' needs to be useful and stimulated, and to maintain pack leadership.

Correcting Chewing, Shredding and Home-Wrecking Behaviours

Even the most conscientious doggy owner who satisfies her pup's canine needs will periodically have to deal with the destruction of at least a few possessions. This could likely happen during the initial imprinting phase, but such behaviour could also erupt from time to time throughout the dog's life. (These later events are most likely to happen when the pooch is naturally exploring boundaries or is going through a stressful period.) Whether you catch your dog in the act or come home to find the home wrecker napping, you must not shrug the behaviour off. Here's what you should do:

1. Take your pup to the scene of the crime and say something like "Not acceptable." Remember to keep your verbalizing simple, firm and calm; don't unleash a diatribe of expletives.

2. If you catch her in the act of chewing or destroying one of your possessions, say, "Leave

it" in a firm, deep tone and take that object away if possible. (Never allow your pup to continue to use one of your trashed possessions as a plaything.) Remember that pups are always held accountable in the canine pack and even young pups are disciplined for overstepping boundaries and engaging in junkyard-dog antics. In the human pack, it's your duty to provide consistent rules of conduct, interrupt potential negative behaviours and provide discipline.

3. Never use the phrase "Stop it" if you catch your pup in the act. As I've already mentioned, the word "Stop" should be reserved for outdoor training—for example, when you are commanding your canine to stay out of traffic. If you bark, "Stop" all the time, your pooch will get used to it, and it won't carry the weight and urgency required when you need to use it outside—especially if your pup is off-leash.

4. Give your pup one of her toys, so she understands that it's quite fine for her to rip away at *her own* playthings. But don't engage in any play or communication with your pup for fifteen minutes. Stay within eyeball range so you can monitor her for any continued bad behaviours, but make a point of doing your own thing and, most especially, don't stage a meltdown! That will only send more mixed messages, especially for a pup

starved of her canine needs who's learned that she has no choice but to engage in negative behaviours in order to get human attention.

If your pup is a repeat homewrecker, it's essential that you address her bad behaviour a.s.a.p. The steps I just outlined might seem simple—and they are—but they're effective because they balance out your relationship. Yes, puppies need to be taught consistent household rules, but a destructive nature in young canines often stems from lack of exercise, understimulation, loneliness and boredom. In other words, neglect. Respect is a two-way street, and you need to acknowledge your role in your dog's bad

MORE PLAY, LESS STRESS

Behavioural scientists endorse playing tug games and retrieval games to motivate and reward dogs during training[10] and also to improve bonding and social skills. Studies have found that playing games like tug and fetch decreased combativeness and competitiveness, enhanced dogs' cooperative skills[11] and even lowered the level of stress chemicals in the brain.[12]

Given the opportunity to play, dogs were often more likely to avoid conflicts and were more interactive and less possessive with toys than dogs who'd had less playtime. Dogs that engaged in less playtime were more likely to misunderstand play cues and show fear or avoidance behaviours.

Researchers have also studied mouthing pups between eight and sixteen weeks of age[13] and found that after three years, they were *no more likely* to be aggressive than young non-mouthing pups.

habits in order to correct them. I know I sound a broken record, but with consistent leadership, daily exercise and new stimuli, your pup won't have the time or inclination to wreck anything!

The Tug O' War Game

So many dogs I've met have developed home-wrecking behaviours or food-related aggressions simply because they were never given the opportunity to learn one important lesson — that is, that they need to respect human possessions and give them back when asked. The Tug O' War Game is a simple and fun way to teach your pup the rules of conduct while also stimulating his smarts and reminding him that Two Legs means business. And this all happens by teaching your dog to release any object on command.

This exercise will also train your pooch to respect human hands so he never bites the hand that feeds him — or any human flesh, especially children's. With consistent "chew training," your pup will also learn not to indulge in possession- and territory-related aggressions. And there's another benefit to this exercise: it will help your pup with the teething process.

Some people doubt the usefulness of tug o' war and think that it instigates aggression. But for domestic and wild canines, it's a natural social game, and it's easily adaptable to interspecies play. Have fun and get to it!

1. Get down on the floor with your pup and a tug-friendly toy like a rope toy, a Kong or an old towel.

2. As with all training and bonding exercises, don't engage in verbal diarrhea! Keep the talk to a minimum to make sure that every word counts.

3. Hold the object out in front of your pup and say, "Get it" in an upbeat, enthusiastic tone.

4. Play tug with your pup for at least thirty seconds.

5. Then say, "Ouch" in a high-pitched tone, as if you were in pain. Yes, you heard me right. This is the one time when you can and should use a high-pitched, squeaky tone: to signal that you're in pain, or pretending to be for training purposes. Make it count. Say it only once, with a lot of gusto.

6. Did your pup release the object? Or did she just look up at you in surprise? If your pup didn't release the object, pinch the top of her ear until she lets out an ouch-like, high-pitched sound and instinctively releases the object.

7. Take the object back.

8. Repeat the exercise, and when you say, "Ouch," your pup should release.

9. If she doesn't release the object, say, "Leave it" in a firm, deep tone. Still not letting it go? Pinch her ear again.

10. Whenever your pup sinks her teeth into your skin, say, "Ouch" in the same, high-pitched tone.

Do this exercise often for the first few weeks your puppy is with you. I also recommend playing tug games regularly with your dog throughout her life to maintain a healthy bond and understanding of the rules of conduct.

Private Dining

Never use a real bone or any canine or human food for tug games. When your pup is eating or chewing on his puppy food or bones from the butcher shop, he's in his own, private comfort zone and doesn't have to do any work or play with you. This is vitally important because if a dog doesn't feel safe and comfortable in his food zone, he can develop food-related aggressions. If you have kids, teach them that the puppy playtime office is closed when your pooch is chowing down.

Hair of the Dog: Grooming Your Pup

Grooming is extremely important, since all pups are groomed by their dog moms from the moment they enter the world. For wild dogs, grooming is an integral part of pack relations because it establishes the mother dog's leadership. It also helps prevent matting and makes it harder for diseases and parasites to wreak havoc on pack health. As I've said before, pack membership is just as important for domestic dogs, so grooming will help you establish and maintain pack leadership with your pup. The level of grooming you'll need to do will depend on the frequency and level of your pet's outdoor activities and the terrain he covers.

Interestingly, different breeds have different grooming habits, so do some research about your pup's breed. A Basenji (bred from stock originating in central Africa) is a meticulous self-groomer and will groom many times a day, in a very structured way, much like a cat. A golden retriever is a slob by comparison and does only a slapdash job. You can figure out your pup's methods by noting how often and how thoroughly he grooms himself every day—especially after a walk, when his coat is sweaty with salt from his sweat. Then, when you go to groom him, follow his lead.

No, I'm not saying lick your dog! Grab a brush and get to it. The brush bristles should be firm, but the length of the bristles will depend on the length of the hairs in your pup's coat. For long-haired pups, the bristles should be more than about a fifth of an inch (half a centimetre) in length. One of the best times to groom your pup is after a good romp. Because he will have burned off a lot of energy, it's more likely that he'll be chill about the whole process. Regular brushing loosens debris from the coat, along with dead fur, insects and parasites. Some pups might need and want to be groomed every day. If that's the case, go for it! But others might clean

themselves more frequently, so in that case, grooming every other day or even once a week would be
fine. However, groom more frequently when your
pup is first with you, because (as mentioned above),
it will help establish your pack dominance.

Some pups take well to being groomed and others
hate it. If your pup dislikes the routine, be sure to
check his body for any open sores or sensitive spots
and take it slow. Leash up your dog before grooming
him and speak in a neutral voice to keep him as relaxed as possible. And start off with a puppy massage
like the ones described in Stage 3. That's a great way
to introduce your pup to being groomed.

Step-by-Step Grooming

1. Treat your pup's spine as if it were a natural
    part on a human's head of hair. From that
    part, you'll brush your dog in four direc-
    tions: east, west, south and north (as out-
    lined in the following steps).

2. Start on the "east" (or your pup's right side,
    at her front legs. Brush downward from her
    spine to her underbelly. Then switch direc-
    tions, brushing upwards. Keep doing this all
    the way along her "east" side, from her front
    legs to her hindquarters.

3. Now, starting at your pup's hindquarters,
    brush north along her spine toward the head
    and chest area, then back to her hindquar-
    ters. Do another brushing from south to
    north (from her hindquarters to her head

and chest area), parallel to her spine, but more toward her east flank. Keep doing this until you've moved all the way to the bottom of her east flank.

4. Now switch to the west (or left) side of your pup and repeat Steps 2 and 3, above.

If her hair is so matted that you can't brush the matts out without inflicting pain, cut them out with scissors right away. If you don't, the matted hairs will just keep growing and pulling at your pup's skin. And this is also very painful. (Be careful with the scissors, though! Don't poke or cut her skin with them. And you can buy scissors with rounded tips to make the grooming a little less precarious—or go to a professional.) A dog's hair becomes matted when hair that has been shed hasn't been brushed away and then mixes with new hair. So do your best to brush away hair that she's already shed.

Puppy's First Bath

I know some dogs who absolutely adore bath time and will even jump in the shower with people. Other dogs can barely tolerate getting near a tub of water for a good cleanup. Chances are you won't know what kind of pup you have until you do the deed a few times. For little pups and small breeds, use a kitchen or laundry room sink.

Make sure the water is at room temperature or just a little warmer. Try to use a nozzle that creates a soft spray and start by getting your pup's paws wet, then gradually move upward. Avoid his head for the first few baths unless your pup takes well to water. Once your pup is wet, give him a gentle massage. Then bring on a gentle, organic dog shampoo and conditioner. Have a towel handy to rub your pup down. Some dogs love getting dried off with a blow dryer but some are freaked out by the process. It will depend on your pet's personality. And since his personality won't emerge for a few months, it would be best not to try blow-drying your pup until then, when he can have a say in the matter.

You won't need to bathe your pup very often during the first few months, but once you start doing a lot of outdoor romps and your pup gets dirty, you'll need to bring on the suds more often. Generally, though, dogs need to be bathed only every six to eight months.

Party On, Puppy: Introducing Your Pup to New Dog and Human Friends

When your pup's about two and a half or three months old, add a few new humans and well-behaved, healthy, vaccinated dogs to the mix so she can learn to socialize. Don't bombard your pup with too many new friends before she's vaccinated, but have some pals over and let the good times roll. Remember that while you have to take your leadership and caregiving responsibilities seriously, the best way to bond with your pooch is to have fun. Don't rush the pace of your initial bonding time by introducing too much training. That might cause stress and anxiety for both you and your pup. Instead, make time for her to meet new people and especially new dog friends that are already speaking the same language.

Like humans, dogs are social creatures, and introducing your canine to other dogs and people as soon as possible makes for a well-balanced pet. Once your pup's personality emerges, you'll be able to appreciate whether your pup is a party animal who likes to have tons of friends or whether she prefers one-on-one encounters or likes to hang back at the dog park to chill with humans. The bottom line is to expose your pup to as many canines and people as possible. For a young pup who hasn't yet had her vaccinations, you won't be able to cruise the dog parks. That's why I recommend starting with a small mixer and inviting only well-behaved, healthy adult dogs. Ideally, the humans will take to your approach to interacting with dogs (including refraining from baby talking and bonding with dogs on the ground, not on the human furniture). If not, be clear about the rules in your home so your pup doesn't have to deal with mixed messages. And be careful not to invite rebel dogs who will teach your pup all the wrong lessons.

When the guests arrive, make sure your pup is on her leash, but don't force her to sit when she's saying her initial hellos to other dogs. That's abnormal greeting behaviour for dogs. They need to stand up and walk around so they can constantly read each other's body language. Typically, dogs will wag their tails when they're receptive, and it's impossible to do that if they're seated. They also need to sniff each other's rumps as part of the fact-checking process. If your pup is in a good mood (and is still well-behaved) after she's mixed with the other dogs, drop the leash, but leave it trailing on the floor in case you have to regain control at any point.

For the most part, well-behaved dogs are the best teachers of canine rules, since they already speak your pup's language. Human translators often tend to just get in the way of a good time, misinterpreting play yelps and growls as aggressive behaviour when in fact, the pooches are probably just exchanging information and chit-chatting. As long as you trust the other dogs at the party, try to leave them to their own devices.

As the days and weeks pass, continue to introduce your pup to new dogs, puppies and people of all ages. Even before vaccination, which I recommend at about two and a half months, you can arrange walks and hikes with other, vaccinated dogs in closed-in areas, free of other animals, and by the time she's three months old, you can start taking your pup to dog parks.

Home Alone: Initial Patience Training

If you have such a busy schedule that you couldn't arrange vacation time during this initial imprinting period, you'll need to consider your pup's well-being while he's at home alone. If you can't take your pup to work with you and if you can't get home during lunch to take your pup out for a short walk and a pee, consider having a friend pop by to tend to your pup or hire a professional dog walker. Whatever your situation, it's ideal to gradually acclimatize your pup to being comfortable on his own. Canines, especially puppies, spend a lot of time sleeping, but if they're anxious or all dialed up when they're alone all day, they'll never learn to be relaxed and cool their heels. Since many pups aren't naturally comfortable when they're alone, I've developed a "patience training" exercise that teaches canines to be patient and calm when you're not around. I'll give you some tips about advanced patience training in Stage 7, but for now, here are the three essential steps of what we'll call "initial patience training."

1. Never make a big deal of your hellos and goodbyes. Don't coddle, kissy-face or engage in long, drawn-out, emotionally wrought physical or verbal messaging when you're coming or going. Canine moms don't prep their pups before they depart, and they don't get all worked up when they return.

2. Condition your pup to being comfortable alone by gradually increasing the amount of time you're away from home by about fifteen minutes each time you leave.

3. When you return after a longer period of time, don't make your return a big, emotionally charged deal. Keep the talk to a minimum and refrain from petting your pup a lot. Reward your pup for his patience by going out for a good, long walk or a romp at the dog park.

STAGE 5

the honeymoon period: street safety training

When your puppy is about two and a half months (eleven weeks) old, you'll likely start to notice that he's bounding along beside you instead of always trailing behind. Ah, what sweet bliss! The "Velcro" pup phase usually continues until a pup is about fifteen weeks old (or three and a half months), but at that point, pups start taking the lead. So this is an ideal time to start teaching your pup, learning more about him and bonding in different ways. First, make sure your pet is fully vaccinated. Once the vaccinations have been completed, you can start street-proofing, using the Sit, Stay, Hustle and Stop exercises I've described later in this chapter. After your pooch has mastered these, you can visit dog parks so that he can talk to other canines in his own language.

While you're doing these street safety training exercises, you'll eventually be able to figure out whether your pup is an instinctual or repetitive learner—though this won't likely be very apparent until he's six months old. Also, your pup might instinctually follow your directions about going to bed or chilling out, but he might need a lot of repetition when it comes to sit-stay training. (This will be especially true if you're doing sit-stay training outdoors with all of its tantalizing distractions.)

Don't rush your pup's street safety training. During this early period, pups tend to follow directions easily, so it's better to maintain consistent training with him in a few areas for the first six months than to get ahead of yourself and load him down and confuse him by cramming in too much training. It's better for him to learn to do a few things very well and get into the habit of following your directions. And enjoy this honeymoon period, because once your pup is seven to nine months old (the terrible twos), he'll start challenging you, and he may also appear challenged by your training.

The Dogged Detective

To properly dial into the canine point of view, think of your pup as a private eye (minus the fedora and trench coat, please), a gumshoe who's trying to solve all the mysteries, crimes and misdemeanours going on around him. Your pup is a curious little ball of fuzz who needs to hound down a whole lot of information. Puppies get so very bored if they spend all of their time in our sterile homes. No wonder some of them get yappy or growl at everything that moves. You don't want that to happen, so get out there and explore the big world and let your pup get on with the investigations that are so important to him. But don't let him venture into the wider world without being street-proofed.

Your pup needs to develop street smarts, and you need to give him the opportunity to do that while still keeping him safe. A dog with street smarts doesn't freak out every time he hears a garbage truck nearby because he's already been exposed to such things. And if you've let him do his fact checking—that is, if he's already discovered what that thing is all about—chances are it won't stress him out. And that means that at six o'clock on Sunday morning, only the sound of the garbage truck will wake you up, not the noise of your dog going ape because that big, loud, stinky villain is back, *again*, to attempt another invasion.

Get the picture? Puppies need a lot of mental stimulation. They're the nosiest busybodies I've ever met. That makes street safety training ideal not just for developing their smarts, but also for giving them the chance to participate in so many of the exciting things going on around them.

The following Sit, Stay, Hustle and Stop training exercises will dial into your pup's smarts and build the foundation for a solid bond and a well-rounded pup. Remember that this is not about old-school obedience training. It's about harnessing your pup's innate smarts and curiosity so that by the end of his first year (and in many cases much sooner), he'll be balanced, street-smart pup who can enjoy the freedom of life off-leash.

Teaching *Sit*

There's that old saying, "Before you can run, you have to learn to walk." Something similar applies to street training dogs. Before they can be street trained, you have to teach them how to sit-stay. A very young pup typically sits as soon as you're stationary, so at this early stage, you don't really have to teach *sit*. But this state of bliss won't last forever. And I recommend practising the "sit" drill anyway because it will allow your pup to become familiar with basic human verbal commands. And that, in turn, will make later intensive training sessions easier.

> Dogs who are able to obey commands have longer lives and need to burn off less energy than dogs who are disobedient. This observation was made during a 2010 Quebec study that found a link between disobedience and aggressive behaviour.[14]

You can do sit-stay training anywhere: on a walk, in the backyard, while you're lacing your shoes just before you and your pup leave home, while running errands—wherever. As for other exercises, it's a good idea to do sit training after your pup has burned off a bit of energy by exercising or playing. But never do the training when she's too tired or on the verge of sleep.

Step-by-Step Sit

1. Leash up your pup and start walking.

2. Stop, and in a firm, neutral tone, say, "Sit," enunciating the "T" clearly.

3. If your pup sits, say, "Good sit" enthusiastically and give her a chest scrunch (see Stage 3 for chest scrunch instructions). Never coo or baby-talk at your pup when you're praising any training-related wins.

4. If your pup doesn't sit, do not continue repeating the command. In fact, *you should never repeat any verbal directive over and over again.* Make the first one count.

If that didn't work, try a *leash-guided sit,* which goes like this:

1. Put the leash on your pup. Then stand directly in front of her and grasp the leash about eight to ten inches (twenty to twenty-five centimetres) from the collar.

2. Tuck your arm in at your side so you're engaging your core, and with your palm turned up, draw up on the leash gently but firmly. As you pull up on the leash, your pup's head will tilt back and her butt will naturally tilt downward, like a teeter-totter.

3. Once your pup is sitting, praise her and wait thirty seconds in a sit-stay. Then start moving around again.

4. Continue with the exercise, mixing up the duration of the sit-stays, increasing and then decreasing the amount of time your pup sits and stays.

5. Stay focused, calm and upbeat. You can't expect your pup to be attentive if you're looking at the clouds, checking your e-mails or tapping your toe and huffing impatiently.

6. If your pup starts to look tired or really distracted, finish with an easy ten-second sit-stay. Wrap every training session with a win.

7. After you wrap each training session, have a brief play session with your pup, or go for a walk if she's still wired for sound.

If your pup resists the leash-guided sit, you have one tenacious dog on your hands. I've met plenty of these characters. With a dog like that, you'll have to be a bit more aggressive and pull the leash up until her front paws are airborne. (It's like putting more weight on one side of the teeter-totter.)

Incorporate sit-stay training into your daily lives until your pup gets the hang of it every time and can sit for a few minutes. Some pups will be able to sit-stay for five minutes with very few training sessions. At this point, they're often ready for off-leash training, which I'll discuss in Stage 7. But don't rush the process, even if your pup learns the ropes quickly. Have fun with it.

Teaching Nonverbal *Sit*

As you progress with daily training, start adding one nonverbal directive after you've directed your pup to sit. For instance, you could add a snap, a hand clap or even a hand gesture. Remember the goal is to do something short, simple, concise and well articulated. You don't need to launch into a game of charades! As you progress, eliminate the verbal command so that your pup starts to respond to the nonverbal command alone. Stay upbeat, keep the messages crystal clear and don't repeat any nonverbal command. If your pup isn't getting either the verbal or the nonverbal command *the first time,* use the leash-guided sit until he understands the request.

Be sure to make the training session shorter or longer, depending on your pup's evolving skill sets and on what type of learner he is (instinctual or repetitive). Don't hammer your dog over the head with a lot of boring training, and bring a healthy level of enthusiasm into your daily sessions.

Teaching *Stay*: Talk to the Hand

Many young pups have short attention spans and need to build up their focus gradually. So don't be too shocked if your pooch is easily distracted and has trouble sustaining a sit-stay (especially when you're training her outdoors). Here's a great technique for honing your pup's attention and ability to sit-stay by teaching "stay" indoors.

1.   Leash your pup and fix the leash handle to the knob of your *closed* front door and stand facing your pup.

2.   Direct your dog to sit, using a verbal "Sit" or snap directive.

3.   Now say "Stay" as you push your hand down toward your pup's head with your palm facing your pup's nose in a "Stop" gesture. (Again, don't say "Stop"; simply use the gesture, which indicates that your pup needs to stay put.) There should be a distance of one inch (two and a half centimetres) between your hand and your pup's head.

4.   Lower your hand and wait for thirty seconds.

5.   If your pup stays put for the duration, praise her with a chest scrunch.

6.   Keep at the exercise until your pup can stay seated for one minute, all the while praising each sit-stay with a chest scrunch.

If your pup starts to break the sit, do not repeat the verbal "Stay" directive, but repeat the "Stop" gesture pronto. Remember that speed and clarity are critical, so be quick and concise with your movements. The goal is to interrupt your pup just before she lifts her butt, so you may have to continue holding your hand out in the "Stop" position for the duration of the sit-stay.

1. Now repeat the exercise, but this time, after you've said, "Stay," open the front door, go outside and take about five steps away from the door. Try to have your pup stay for two minutes.

2. If your pup breaks the stay and gets up, the door will close, or at the very least, the leash will restrict her movement and prevent her from bolting outside.

3. Go back inside and repeat the exercise from the top.

Do this exercise daily for short periods. A pup should be able to sit-stay consistently by the age of three and a half to four months of age. Once you start to have consistent success, do this exercise outdoors and attach the leash to a park bench, a bike rack, a tree or any other secure, stationary device. Never use table or chair legs or anything that your pup has the power to pull. If she breaks from a sit-stay and starts to pull that object behind her, she'll think she's being chased, and that could cause aggression or panic.

And one final, important note: it's essential to do this initial sit-stay training before you start heading to dog parks, practise patience training or begin off-leash training

Teaching *Hustle*, or *Come*

It's a great idea to make sure your pup knows how to "Come" or "Hustle" before you start heading to the dog parks, and especially before you try any off-leash play. Here's a simple exercise to introduce that directive to your pup, starting indoors at home, in your backyard or in any enclosed space (such as a basketball or tennis court).

1.   Direct your unleashed pup to sit. Then stand about three steps away, facing him.

2.   Squatting down on your haunches or getting down on your knees, make an encouraging gesture (such as slapping your hands on your thighs). Then open your arms wide.

3.   When your pup comes running to you, give him a good chest scrunch as a reward.

4.   Repeat the above steps, but gradually increase the distance between you and your pup until you're at least twenty steps apart.

5.   To wrap a session, when your pup runs to you, have a good play romp. This will reward your pup and imprint on his mind the notion that you're a fun caregiver. That way,

whenever you call for your pup to come to you, your pup won't flip you the paw, thinking you and all your orders are, like, such a bummer.

After the first week of teaching, continue facing your pup, squatting down and opening your arms wide, but instead of slapping your thighs, start introducing the verbal command "Come" or "Hustle." (Again, the specific words aren't important as long as they're brief, crystal clear and upbeat. But make sure they're never high-pitched.) If your pup doesn't respond to this verbal command, don't repeat it. Instead, slap your hands on your thighs in an encouraging way. It may take a few sessions for your pup to get the hang of the verbal directive to "Hustle."

Nonverbally Speaking

The "Come" and "Hustle" commands are the most overused human-to-dog orders in the interspecies communication playbook. So try to avoid using any verbal commands during the first few sessions.

Practise this exercise whenever you have some time and always end on a positive, winning note.

Teaching *Stop*

This command is, beyond a doubt, the most important verbal command in the puppy training toolbox. In fact, it will probably help you save your pup's life at least a few times over. It's one of the main reasons I mentioned earlier that you should never say, "Stop" to your pup in other circumstances. Your canine needs to learn to respect and heed the urgency of the "Stop" command more than any other verbal or nonverbal command in the training toolbox. Stop training is especially challenging for many dog owners, in part because they find it difficult to master the quick, concise movements and gestures that go with it. So don't get too stressed out if it takes months for you and your pup to see consistent success with it. (But do note that it's only after your pup has mastered the "Stop" command that she'll be ready for advanced off-leash training.)

Here are the steps to follow in teaching your pup to "Stop":

1. Leash your pup, but let the leash trail on the ground and tell your pup to sit-stay.

2. Stand about two feet (half a metre) away, facing your pup, with your chest out, shoulders back.

3. Direct your pup to "Hustle," but as soon as she starts to move, throw your hand forward in a "Stop" gesture facing her head and say, "Stop" in a firm voice, enunciating the "P" clearly.

4. This mix of the "Stop" gesture and the verbal command should be fluid and quick. Remember that speed and clarity of movement are key.

5.   If your pup continues to move toward you, allow your palm to make contact with her snout if necessary. Chances are your pup will stop moving at this point because she won't have the space to do anything else. There's no need to praise her at this initial stage.

Now take another step backward and repeat the process. Ideally, your pup will stop on a dime. If she does that, reward her with a chest scrunch. If she continues to charge at you, keep your hand braced in the "Stop" position and let her make contact with your hand. But don't repeat the command and don't move your hand! Keep your "Stop" gesture firm so she knows you mean business and you're not going to give in to her. Then pick up the leash, guide her back to her starting point and begin the process from the top again. Gradually increase the distance between you and your dog until you're about twenty feet (six metres) away and she's stopping on a dime as soon as you say "Stop." And remember that you should not say "Stop" when your pup is doing something you don't want her to do. Instead, use words like "No" or "Leave it" if she misbehaves.

Hit the Streets:
Initial Street Safety Training

It's important to train your pup to sit-stay, hustle and stop, but don't get hung up on enforcing long sit-stays or teaching your pup to stop on a dime before you start street safety training. As I've said before,

Umbilical Do-Si-Do

If, when you have your pup on umbilical, you need to move her from one side of you to the other, guide her so she goes behind you, never in front. That would be a tripping hazard! Grab the leash just below your waist loop and slide it in the direction needed to let your pup move over to the opposite side. This might seem awkward at first, but it will become a fluid movement with time.

your goal is not to create a robot dog, but to let your pup have fun while you offer consistent leadership. And dogs really flourish when they can get out there and explore the world. So expose your pup to as much as possible under your watchful eye. My training philosophy is always about incorporating interactive and fun training into your daily mix.

Start in a quiet neighbourhood with sidewalks and take it easy at first. Gradually dial up the level of traffic exposure as your pup's confidence and abilities increase. In your initial forays into the wider world, make sure your pup is on umbilical so he can stay close to you and you'll be sure that he's safe. Approach this exercise with a good attitude, solid posture and a sense of adventure. If you're nervous or anxious, your pup will notice and feed off of it. Take in your world as you think your pup might see it, through smells and sounds and movements. Practise alertness and mindfulness until it comes naturally.

Step-by-Step Street Safety Training

1. Check to make sure your pup's collar fits properly (one thumbnail length should separate the two collar rings when the chain

is taut and triangulated). Then get into umbilical mode.

2. Position yourself on the street side of the sidewalk with your pup on the inside.

3. Be mindful of your body language. Walk assertively, with your shoulders back and your body's core engaged.

4. As you approach the first curb, make sure you're between your pup and the busiest street in the intersection.

5. Once you're about six feet (two metres) from the intersection, direct your pup to sit with a firm, calm verbal command: "Sit." Don't forget to enunciate the "T" clearly. Or use a finger snap or whatever sound you've trained your pup to respond to.

6. Take note of any street traffic and other pedestrians around you before you take that first step toward the curb.

7. As you step off the curb, take three quick steps onto the street. The initial speedy pace will strengthen your pup's attentiveness and dial him in to your movements.

8. After that third step, slow your pace down a bit as you cross the street. Don't dilly-dally, but don't race either.

9. As you approach the opposite curb, pick up your pace again for three full steps until you're safely on the sidewalk. Again, this increased speed will signal to your pup that he needs to be attentive and respectful of your movements.

10. Continue walking, repeating the above instructions at each curb.

As you become more agile with street training in quiet neighbourhoods, dial up the level of exposure to street traffic by introducing your pup to busier streets and neighbourhoods. View each positive training session as a building block toward giving your pup the pleasure of being off-leash trained.

YOU'RE IN CONTROL!

Always remember that your dog will respond most positively if your body language is positive. Be aware of what's going on around you, but maintain strong, controlled body language. If you're hesitant, fearful or anxious, you'll saddle your pup with stress and anxiety. This, in turn, will have one or another effect on your dog: it will either force him into taking on the leadership position or it will make him nervous and jittery. Neither of these extremes is healthy, and your pup might even toggle back and forth from one extreme to another, depending on his mood and the situation. Don't encourage these extreme behaviours. If you're a reliable, assertive dog owner, your pup will follow your lead all the time. And that will make your daily walks enjoyable bonding experiences.

Then you can embrace all sorts of new experiences happily and safely, and your pup won't be tempted to sink to manipulative tactics, constantly pushing the envelope to test your leadership.

Vehicle Safety:
Entering and Exiting Cars and Trucks

In the next few sections, we'll be heading to the dog park, but not everyone is lucky enough to be able to walk there. Plenty of dog owners have to drive their pooch to the local doggy watering hole. So before we head off for your puppy's first day in the park, let's walk through some vehicle-proofing basics. Parking lots are giant booby traps for pups and dogs. Combine that with a pup who's raring to get out to hang with the other dogs, and you have a disaster waiting to happen. But take heart. You can minimize the hazards with a few safeguarding tips.

Seven Essential Steps to Vehicle Safety

1. Always park your vehicle so that its doors open in a direction opposite to street or parking lot through routes. That way your pup will be as far away as possible from traffic when he's coming and going. Whether it's your home driveway or a busy parking lot, this typically means backing your vehicle into a parking space.

2. Make sure your pup is on his leash before you leave home for car trips and just before

you head to the parking lot after a romp at the dog park. Remember that even if you're on a quiet street, your pup could bolt off at any time and be hit by another vehicle, especially in parking lots. (As usual, consistency is key at all times—so remember to be consistent about attaching that leash!)

3.   Young pups are often too small to leap in and out of vehicles on their own. In fact, if they try to do that, the stress on their spines and joints can cause damage over time. So for the first few months, you'll be picking up your pup unless he's of such a large breed that it's easy for him to leap into your vehicle. But after that, it's a bad idea to continue picking up your pup or adult dog at any time.

Puppy Pickup Reminder

You already learned, in Stage 3, how to pick up your pup. But it's so important not to damage his young body that the method is worthy of repetition here.

1.   Squat down and slide one hand between the front legs and under the chest area until your hand is palming and supporting the puppy's rib cage and front region.

2.   Put your other hand at the top of his hind limbs, just below the tail and butt. This way

his back region will be supported, and your hand can stabilize both his body and his legs.

3. Never compress your pup's spine. The goal is to keep the body long.

4. As with lifting anything, bend and lift with your knees and keep your back straight.

5. Never allow your pup to enter or exit the vehicle before you're ready. Direct him to sit before you open the vehicle door and invite your pup inside with a "Hustle" or a "Let's go."

6. Make sure your pup is on-leash by the time you're at least fifty yards (fifty metres) away from the parking lot.

7. Never allow your pup to sit in the front seat and never, ever let your dog sit on your lap while you're driving. Some people buckle their dogs in the back seat. I typically let my dogs sit on the floor in front of the back seat.

8. Keep the windows in your vehicle closed or open just a crack. We all know how much dogs love sticking their heads out of windows to pick up the daily news. But there are all kinds of debris and insects in the air that could lodge in your pup's eyes and potentially cause severe damage or even blindness. A dog's head could also collide with another vehicle, causing death or terrible injury.

The Dog Park: Positive Vibes

I know I sound like a broken karaoke machine, but the ideal way to maximize positive dog training is to mix it up with a lot of play and rewards. Socializing at the dog park is the ideal way to complement any training. It's the canine equivalent of a cocktail party, the weekly book club, the dance club or any gathering where we have the chance to socialize with our own species. It's up to us to provide our pups with many opportunities to chat, play, dance and romp with other dogs. Any well-balanced dogs that your pup will meet at such jamborees are the best teachers of canine etiquette, and consistent interdog mingling is the best method for preventing and correcting antisocial behaviours like aggression and separation anxiety.

Your pup won't necessarily click with every single dog she meets at the dog park. Just like the way it is with humans, the chemistry just isn't there sometimes, so don't sweat it if she doesn't take to a particular pooch. Too often, however, the humans are the issue because they get nervous before the dog-to-dog encounter even begins. Your dog will pick up that negative energy, especially if your body language isn't confident and relaxed. If you're anxious, your pup will either internalize your anxiety and make it her own or she'll feel the need to step into the leadership role and become the dog park bully. Don't let either of those behaviours emerge!

People also tend to misinterpret dog park growls or gestures. I've seen so many well-intentioned people misread doggy cues and bust up a perfectly normal play session. How would you feel if someone butted into your conversations and dragged you away by the scruff? Whatever the behaviour, we should never punish our dogs for expressing how they feel. Remember that they're talking in dogspeak, and the last thing they need is an amateur human translator charging in and getting the messages all mixed up.

Of course, you do need to keep in mind the attitudes and traits of other people and their dogs. You'll meet many types of humans and canines at the dog park, and there's no guarantee that all of them will be stellar, well-balanced individuals. So as you approach the park, assess the goings-on around you. Keep your pup leashed, but have a relaxed, positive attitude. Make eye contact with other people and view every opportunity to chat as a combination of a fact-finding mission and a chance to make some new two- and four-legged friends. (The facts you find might include learning whether other people and their dogs are friendly and habituated to other dogs and pups or whether they're wound up tighter than a yo-yo.)

Look out for potentially negative canine body language that could indicate aggression. For instance, a dog that seems to be standing at attention with his head raised high and his neck extended or the hair on his neck and back raised is likely not a happy camper. Some dogs will tuck their tails between their legs to indicate fear or aggression, but sometimes aggressive dogs will display no obvious negative behaviours. Be extra cautious with children at the dog park. Make sure you ask parents if it's okay to introduce your pup to a child *before* your pup and that child start reaching out to each other.

PUPPIES ARE PEOPLE MAGNETS

We all know that puppies attract a lot of attention, and now there's evidence to prove it.[15] Italian researchers recruited handlers to go out in public leashed up to either a puppy or a small adult dog while a remote camera tracked the reactions of passing pedestrians. Those pedestrians were then polled by another researcher with fifteen questions meant to gauge the pedestrians' responses. The puppies caused a much bigger stir than the small adult dogs, eliciting more positive emotions like tenderness (64.9 percent vs. 29.1 percent) and lower indifference (8.2 percent vs. 20.5 percent).

These strangers also showed a greater tendency to stop and engage with the puppies. People were also twice as likely to want to chat with the two-legged handlers, proving that dogs are a catalyst for human-to-human contact. And, interestingly, it wasn't just size that made a dog appealing; it was that puppy magnetism at work!

If your young pup has yet to be spayed or neutered, ask the owner of any prospective buddy whether that dog has already been fixed. If not, keep your pup away! If you don't, either you or the owner of the other dog may end up dealing with an unwanted pregnancy.

The Step-by-Step Dog Park Meet-and-Greet

1. Once you've figured out that another dog is a good match, drop your pup's leash, but let it drag on the ground in case you need to come to his assistance and regain control.

2.   Give your dog a firm pat on the side and in an enthusiastic tone, say, "Go play."

3.   Leave your pup and the other chosen good dog matches to their own devices. Resist hovering over them while they're playing, and make sure you don't bark away at them.

Give your pup lots of time to play and bond with the other pups and dogs. And while they're doing that, take the opportunity to assess any emerging or established personality traits, such as whether your pup is a party animal or more reserved and laid back.

Listen to all the dog chatter and take note of how your pup engages in conversation. Some dogs are chatterboxes that like to growl, yelp and bark a lot, while others "speak" sparingly. Analyze your pup's facial and body language so you can get to know his typical dog-to-dog interactions. Once you understand what's normal behaviour for him, you'll be able to identify any abnormal behaviours such as aggression or anxiety. Take note of the way your pup and other dogs gesture and engage with each other. Here are some possible behaviours you might observe:

- *The play bow.* Facing each other and crouching, with their butts arched upward, their heads drawn forward and low, and their paws splayed forward. This is the canine equivalent of a curtsy.

- *The tail wag.* This happens when they're happy or dialed in. But look out for dogs who wag their tails and act dominantly. All dogs wag their tails to communicate, but some communicate aggression this way.

- *The submissive roll.* When a pooch rolls onto his back, belly-up, he's likely a submissive dog signaling that he's game to play with a dominant dog.

- *Playing with toys.* A dog might hold her paws over a ball or stick as if to say, "Mine. I'm not sharing." Or she might place her toy beside or in front of another dog's paws as if to say, "Hey, buddy, try it yourself."

When it's time to leave the park, crouch down, open your arms wide at your sides and in an enthusiastic tone, say, "Come, Charlie" or whatever your pup's name is. Or if you prefer, stick to the more generic verbal commands like "Hustle" or "Let's go." The key is to keep your voice firm but upbeat.

If your pup comes to you immediately, congrats! Your stay-training sessions are paying off. Give her a chest scrunch and then pick up the leash to re-establish control. If your pup continues to play with other dogs, don't repeat the verbal command. Be considerate of the fact that your pup is having a blast, and let her play for a few more minutes before you attempt another verbal directive, such as "Hustle." If your pup continues to ignore you, approach her and pick up her leash to guide her away. Don't be disappointed if she doesn't immediately get the hang of your verbal command when it's time to leave the dog park. Pups need a lot of practice with this one, and it probably won't start sinking in until she's three months of age at the earliest.

As the days, weeks and months pass, take your pup to a variety of different dog parks and socialize her by visiting other places such as a sidewalk café or by taking her on a walk downtown. A dog who visits the same dog park every day can become territorial or just plain bored with the same old sights, sounds and smells. To prevent that and also to increase your pup's confidence level, provide a mix of places and dog parks for dog-to-dog socializing.

As your pup matures, you will get a better sense of whether she's typically a dominant canine pack member or a submissive pack member. Different dog mixes and different settings will probably tip the balance in one direction or the other, but well-balanced, well-socialized dogs that get a healthy mix of exposure to a variety of dog parks and dog-to-dog situations will be able to gauge the situation and tweak their behaviours to suit that specific pack mix in a satisfactory way. Unless your pup or another dog exhibits dangerous behaviour, such as biting, butt out of the dog parties and let your pup develop her own understanding of her place in the dog pack.

Heat Stroke

Ah, the dog days of summer. We all love 'em. But extreme heat exposure can be downright deadly to your pet. A dog falls victim to heat stroke when her body temperate goes above 105°F (41°C), and this happens most often when a dog is left in a vehicle without adequate ventilation. It can also happen when a dog is left outside in humid weather without shade or when she's overexercised. And a dog can be felled by heat stroke even on relatively cool days, when the temperature is about 70°F (21°C). Other risk factors for heat stroke include obesity or diseases affecting the pet's airways. And short-nosed breeds (like pugs, bulldogs and some terriers) can be predisposed to heat stroke because they have trouble panting, which reduces body temperature.

Look out for these initial symptoms: distress, restlessness and excessive panting. Many people wonder about the term "excessive panting," but by this point in your relationship with your pup, you should have had plenty of time to gauge what's normal and what's excessive.

Urgent signs of heat stroke include excessive drooling from the nose and mouth, gums turning bluish purple or bright red and unsteadiness on the feet. That could mean your pup's not getting enough oxygen.

Severe symptoms include the inability to stand, and in severe cases, a dog can develop DIC (disseminated intravascular coagulation), which causes abnormal bleeding and blood clotting, or acute kidney failure, which requires hospitalization. In these extreme cases, studies have found that heat stroke has a 50 percent mortality rate for dogs, so it's important to take preventive measures.

If signs of heat stroke appear—even early ones—act fast. Get your pup out of the situation to a shaded spot or a cool indoor area. If you have a fan or air conditioner, turn it on. If possible, take his rectal temperature and record it. Put cool, wet towels over the back of his neck, at the armpits and in the groin area. Wet the pup's ear flaps and paws with cool water. Never use ice or very cold water. (This will actually cause a reaction that holds the heat in and slows the dog's ability to cool down.) Then take your pup to the vet for emergency care.

On really hot and humid days, it's best to limit your outdoor activities to shaded streets and parks; wooded, cooler places; and places where you have access to rivers, lakes and water. That way you can cool your pup down regularly. Take water and a collapsible water dish with you and be extra careful not to let a young pup's fragile paw pads have too much contact with cement, asphalt, sand and stones.

PUPPY ATTACHMENT

According to scientists at the Budapest-based Family Dog Project,[16] puppies will show attachment to their owners even at the tender age of sixteen weeks. But they don't show attachment to unfamiliar humans at that age. The scientists hypothesized that this attachment ability "not only allows for developing a close relationship to a different species but it also operates for an extended period into adult life." They also noted that "the attachment system in dogs could serve as the scaffolding on which many forms of complex social behaviour between dogs and humans can develop." For those of you who have adopted adult dogs, take heart. They found that "even socially deprived adult dogs show such attachment behaviour after a short social handling by an unfamiliar person."

Puppy-Friendly Toys

After your pup has been vaccinated, head out to the pet store to choose three new toys for chewing, for playing tug and for fetch and retrieval. With the store owner's permission, spread a bunch of toys around your pup and let her follow her own nose to figure out her preferences. But please limit the number of toys to three. Canines don't need an abundance of props and gadgets. The goal is to have three different kinds, to satisfy their basic needs.

Replace the old toys with your pup's new toys she's chosen. Then, as your pup matures, replace a toy after it's worn out or if your pup starts to lose interest in it.

STAGE 6

who's the boss? assertive leadership skills

When your pup turns about three and a half months old, she'll start to take the lead. At least she'll try to! And by the time your pup is four months old, you'll start to feel a strain on the leash during walks. Even though I love this stage because it proves how smart and curious pups are when it comes to exploring boundaries, pulling on the leash isn't acceptable canine behaviour. It might seem adorable and harmless, especially with featherweight, small-breed pups, but those of you with large-breed pups know it's serious business, and you have the aching shoulders to prove it.

By the time your pup is seven months old, she'll have had ample time to assess her place in the pack, and if you haven't been following all the training and leadership methods described in this book—or, worse, if you've shirked her canine needs for exercise, mental stimulation and socialization with other dogs, your omissions and inconsistencies will come back to haunt you. And without proper direction, by the time your puppy is one year old, she'll be ready to stage a hostile takeover of your household!

That's why I always emphasize the importance of asserting and maintaining your leadership *before* your dog attempts that *coup d'état* and before she develops all sorts of rebellious behaviours that are so much harder to fix in dog adulthood. This is important from a behavioural standpoint, but also, by showing your pup that you're the leader, you'll be giving her the opportunity and encouragement to let her unique personality bloom as a stress-free, well-balanced member of your pack.

The instinctual behaviours of your puppy's breed usually start becoming more apparent between three and nine months of age. Have you started to notice that your herding breed of pup is constantly nipping at your pant leg or trying to herd people? Has your shepherd pup assumed a corner office at the front window and is he now barking at anything and everything that passes by? Maybe your beagle has started fixating on squirrels? These new habits might seem cute right now, but once your pup is physically mature (at about eighteen months or so) and has a much more powerful body and jaw, these behaviours can become dangerous—not to mention annoying! I'll show you how to nip these potential problems in the bud now by giving you more advanced interruption techniques and introducing you to canine-friendly correction techniques that mimic your pup's innate need for rules and boundaries.

You might also start to notice certain pet peeves or sensitivities emerging. They could be triggered by vacuum cleaners, toilet paper, the garbage truck, the full moon, stormy weather or specific sounds (such as a certain musical pitch). I love it! These issues show us the great extent to which dogs are tuned in to anything and everything around them and how doggedly inquisitive they are. I'll help you see these reactions from your pup's unique point of view.

Alpha Test

Assessing canine dominance is a complex endeavour, and it's something I prefer to do only after I've spent at least a few hours with a dog and his human pack. But there are some easy-to-identify signs that a pup thinks he's on the fast track to becoming your pack CEO or that he's already stolen your job. It's ideal to act preventively to ensure that doesn't happen. If it has, you'll have to do so much hard work reassuming leadership status. Here are some signs that your puppy is polishing his résumé or has already moved into the executive suite.

- He chills, sleeps and jumps up on the human furniture in the household.

- He bolts to be first at the front door when guests visit.

- He barks excessively or growls deeply to dominate or protect possessions or members of the household.

- He jumps up on any humans.

- He tries to lead you when you arrive or depart, especially through the front door.

- He always wants to be in the lead at any transition point, such as an elevator, stairway, escalator, gate or vehicle.

- He always pulls at the leash, even after a good outdoor romp and a few sides of canine interactions en route.

- He tries to manipulate you by displaying exaggerated signs of submission as soon as you even attempt to assert your leadership. These fake-out submissions include shrieking an equivalent of "Ouch" when you dethrone him from *your* bed or favourite armchair; twirling around in circles when you try to clip on the leash for a walk; and dropping down or rolling over like a drama queen at the dog park after he's had adequate socialization time and you need to wrap it up.

Alpha Think: Embrace the Spotlight

Whether your pup exhibits any of the above alpha signs or whether she's still assessing your leadership

PACK STATUS

Behaviour scientists at the Family Dog Project in Budapest contend that dogs who have high-quality bonds with their owners perform better in training tasks and will look to their owner to solve problems, thanks, in part, to their canine smarts and "willingness to assume a subordinate role in their social group."[17] This research highlights just how important it is for us humans to embrace the leadership role in the interspecies pack, by establishing and maintaining consistent rules of conduct and teaching our pups how to acclimatize to the human pack.

capabilities, you don't want to let your puppy get used to taking the lead. That's something pups have the right to do only at appropriate times, such as tugging at the leash when they need outdoor exercise or socialization or when they need to use the outdoor "potty."

Many people find it challenging to embrace their leadership status because they think roles like "dominant" and "submissive" are far too extreme and condescending to their canine buddies. They don't think of themselves as domineering when they tell their human kids they have to eat their veggies before they get any dessert or they have to finish their homework before they play soccer. And they don't think of themselves as iron-fisted bosses when they show a new employee the ropes at work. They're not mean, maniacal coaches when they teach people how to play a sport, learn to dance or play poker. Yet as soon as I tell some of my clients that they'll have to learn how to physically manage their dogs by controlling their pace, using confident body language and inter-rupting and correcting negative behaviours like leash pulling or couch poaching, they become hesi-tant, unsure or even oppositional.

If you feel this way remember to picture your pup's canine elders—the moms, the sibling teach-ers, the pack teachers and leaders. These dogs em-brace their leadership positions and will quickly flag and call foul on a pup's canine misbehaviours, pri-marily through physical movements. A dog pack leader is a bit like that conductor at the symphony, who uses crisp, fast, assertive movements to direct all the players. The majority of us have no clue what they're doing; it's as if they're speaking their own pri-vate language.

When a puppy reaches the developmental stage at which she starts to take the lead, we need to har-ness and hone our dogspeak skills by borrowing methods from the canine playbook: tuning up our use of assertive, clear, concise body language, as well as minimizing our verbal methods of communica-tion. Remember that an ideal pack leader takes sug-gestions from his subordinates, and your subordinate (your pup) is actually asking you this: "Learn to speak canine and *show* me what you want and need me to do." Umbilical is the ideal technique for tap-ping into your dogspeak skills, but now that your pup is quicker, stronger and more dexterous and has started taking the lead, it's time to ramp up your level of assertive body movement with advanced umbilical training.

Advanced Umbilical

Start this training session after your pup has had at least one adequate outdoor walk and her physical and mental needs have been met. She's had a chance to pick up the daily news and chit-chatted with at least a few other dogs. The goal, as usual, is not to create a robot dog but to encourage your pet to communicate her needs and to remind you to respect those needs by fulfilling them. I recommend doing these umbilical sessions two or three times a day for about twenty minutes each time. As I mentioned when I introduced umbilical training in Stage 4, you can do these exercises at home too, while you're moving around the house. But let's start with outdoor umbilical so you can hone your pup's focus in the midst of numerous outdoor distractions.

Step-by-Step Advanced Umbilical

Before you start, check the size of your pup's Martingale collar. (For the leash correction method to work, you must use a Martingale collar.) Inspect all the connection points on the collar and leash to make sure everything's in working order.

1. Get into umbilical while you're inside your home.

2. Make sure you're in the lead when you go out your front door and through any transition points such as gates, elevators and stairwells.

3. If your pup starts to take the lead as you're walking through a doorway, move quickly to close that door and place your pup in a sit-stay for about twenty seconds before you open the door again. (You might have to repeat this little exercise a few times before your pup gets the idea that you're in control of all movements.)

4. Move with assurance and good posture, with your shoulders relaxed, chest out and your core engaged.

5. Don't touch the leash. Pretend it's not there.

6. Find your way to a sidewalk where you can walk in a straight line. (You'll see why in a minute.)

7. If at any point your pup steps ahead of you, change directions and increase your speed. Continue doing so for a few minutes, walking back and forth on the sidewalk.

8. After a few minutes of the above, if your pup still gets in your way, don't step or move around her. Keep moving in a straight line. Your pup needs to learn that she's not a piece of furniture that you have to navigate around. She also needs to learn that it's *her* responsibility to get out of *your* way. Once she realizes this, she'll clearly understand that you're in control of all movements.

As you're walking, allow your leg and foot to make contact with your pup's body if she gets in the way. Don't bunt your pup around like a football, but exert the pressure needed to guide her out of your path. With larger pups and mature dogs, your speed should be quicker paced. You don't want to step down on a canine's toes, but let your foot make enough contact that there's very slight pressure on the paws—or for tiny pups, get close enough that your foot is at least brushing the hairs on his paws. Whenever you find *yourself* navigating around your pup to accommodate him, your pup just scored a win. Each time that happens, go back to the beginning of the sidewalk and start again.

9. The next time your pup takes the lead, stop immediately.

10. "Stop" means no shuffling, no moving at all. Keep your feet braced and your stance the width of your hips.

   Did your pup stop immediately? If so, great! Continue moving. If your pup continued walking, causing *any* strain on the leash, you will need to kick into action immediately and implement a leash correction. I'll discuss the leash correction method in the next section and then provide a step-by-step exercise.

Leash Leadership

My leash correction method has never failed to get a puppy's attention. It harnesses his curiosity and instinctual cravings and helps him learn to be a law-abiding dog citizen who's in sync with his pack. As you now know, canines have all sorts of subtle methods for expressing leadership, maintaining respect and teaching pups the canine rules. In dogspeak, that usually means getting physical. Dogs rarely use brute force to highlight their authority. Instead, they use body movements and quick, short-duration gestures to maintain control. In the *human* world, pups need to be taught to understand that we can manage and take care of them—or else they'll feel as if they're forced to take over that position themselves.

For domestic dogs, the leash is an extension of their human pack member's leadership. So for you to communicate your authority and trustworthiness as a leader, the ideal method is the leash correction (it's better than verbal instruction). It "says," in crystal-clear, easy-to-understand language, "Hey, doggy! You need to pay attention to me because I'm your leader, your caregiver, your coach and your buddy. I've got your back here in the human world, and that means I have to teach you how to be safe, well-balanced and content." Don't force your pup to tune you out by excessively chattering, barking, begging or yelling.

This leash correction method is the ideal way to steal your pup's attention away from all the fantastic distractions of life and dial him into you. And it won't cause your puppy any physical harm. But if you're a doubter about the level of physicality it involves, try the method out on your hand first or get a friend to strap the collar onto your leg and then do the leash correction.

You must use a Martingale collar with this technique because as I mentioned earlier, it's designed for quick-release action. And don't be disappointed if it doesn't work smoothly right away. You might need to do a fair bit of practice before you can really make the technique sing. Don't be tough on your dog if it doesn't go according to plan right away. But be a bit tough on yourself: make sure you follow every step by the book until the process comes naturally.

Step-by-Step Leash Correction

Start off by moving around on umbilical for a while, and when you stop, be sure that your feet are firmly planted and your core is solid. As soon as your pup steps ahead of you and the leash strains, proceed with the following steps:

1. Grab the leash between your thumb and index finger, palm facing up, and quickly draw up on the leash. (Note that your shoulder shouldn't be controlling the upward movement. It should remain square, just as with the leash-guided sit. Note too that your motion should be faster and briefer than in the leash-guided sit.)

2. Think of the motion as a quick snap and release. It's not about power; it's about speed and momentum and the element of surprise.

3. Release the leash immediately. The entire leash correction process should be over before you've had a chance to count a second-long "One banana." It should look like a quick, fluid upward snap and release of the leash.

4. Do this leash correction once and only once. Don't "ring the church bells" by doing one yank after another after another. Make the one leash correction count.

5. Your pup should immediately stop and look up at you as if to say, "Wow, you got my attention. You've proven that you can physically manage my movements. I'm dialed in to you. What's next?"

6. If your pup continues to plough ahead, yanking on the leash, don't shuffle ahead. Keep your feet planted where you are. And resist the temptation to continue pulling upward, straining the leash. This is not a fishing expedition. Your pup's front paws shouldn't come off the ground.

7. Instead, do another lightning-fast leash correction and release.

8.   Even a tenacious dog should now stop and look at you.

9.   Start moving again. Walk for another twenty paces and repeat the above exercise.

10. Incorporate a verbal "Sit" directive into the mix. But make sure you stop and plant your feet before you tell your pup to sit. If you make that request while you're still moving, you'll be sending a mixed message that will confuse your canine. (It's a bit like continuing to pull on the reins when you want a horse to stop. That will confuse the horse or make the horse think you want her to turn around. Instead, one crisp pull and release on those reins means "Stop.")

11. When your pup sits, be sure to praise her with a chest scrunch.

12. Whenever your pup gets ahead and causes a leash strain, do another quick, brief, concise leash snap and release.

13. Continue moving around for different durations of time, switching back and forth between longer and shorter durations and replacing your verbal "Sit" command with a leash correction snap command.

Some pups will be stellar students and will respond to your leash correction immediately. Other

You're the Boss

Don't be spotlight shy when it comes to embracing your leadership authority. Be assertive, consistent and in control. Every hesitation or wavering will be interpreted as a failure in dogspeak. You don't want your pup to see you as an embarrassed stumblebum because she'll then think, "Hmm, Two Legs doesn't have my back. Now I have to step into the role of having his back." Your pup will feel compelled to take the leadership position, and that will only lead to a pile of losses for both species.

pups are more tenacious and will resist authority whenever they can. If that's the case, don't lose your cool. Maintain patience and consistency while your pup learns to be dialed into your movements all the time.

The key aspects of the leash correction method are speed, crispness, brevity and consistency. It's like a towel snap. The goal is to be playful, using the element of surprise to catch your pup off guard. With a towel snap, you need just the right degree of strength, speed and economy of movement. Too little speed and momentum and that towel will just wave in the breeze. Too much and it will become a hurtful whip. Remember that the leash correction method is not about using brute force against your pup or treating him like a fish at the end of a reel by continually yanking at the leash until he's flip-flopping in the air. Just like the use of spare, concise verbal language, this correction is most effective when it's done once, and only once, each time you need to get your pup's attention.

A canine's mouth moves seven times faster than the typical movement of the human hand, so if you're trying to mimic your puppy's pack friends, you'll have to increase your speed and dexterity. That way you'll not only capture your pup's attention, but he'll be captivated by your momentum and your managerial fortitude.

The Toe Tap Game

The Toe Tap Game is a fun way to complement advanced umbilical training and to reinforce the fact that you're in the driver's seat when it comes to controlling your pup's movements. Again, this exercise is not about exerting dominant authority so you can power-trip just for the heck of it. It's about safeguarding your domestic pup against potential hazards of the human world, particularly anything on wheels. (Canines are especially tempted to get in the way of, or chase, things like bikes, lawn mowers, Rollerblades, skateboards, strollers and vehicles.) Pups and dogs also tend to get underfoot a lot, so they can be

Tripping Out

Falls are the leading cause of nonfatal injuries treated at emergency rooms in the United States according to a U.S. report[18] that found that over eighty-six thousand human injuries yearly involved cats and dogs. Eighty-eight percent were canine-specific, and human females were two times more likely to be injured than males. Vets recommended dog obedience training to prevent these accidents.

tripping hazards for humans, especially around children and on stairs, on recreational paths and at transition points, like doorways and gates. That's one reason why it's so important for Two Legs to *always* be in the lead. (The only exception to this rule happens when a pup has been off-leash trained and they've earned the privilege to lead their owners occasionally.)

The Toe Tap Game is also a great way to bond and to stimulate your pup's blossoming personality and coordination skills. As puppies mature, it's important to ramp up the physicality of our interactions and the games we play with them. That's why the Toe Tap Game is great for maturing dogs. It takes the Paw-Grappling Game from Stage 3 to a new level, since you'll be using your feet (instead of your fingers and hands) as paws. As dogs mature, their physical tussling and playing become more assertive, sure-footed and bold when they mix with other mature pups and adult dogs. Similarly, this game represents a step up in physicality as compared to the Paw-Grappling Game.

Here's how it goes:

1.   Get down on the ground, outside or inside, and start playing with one of your pup's favourite tug or chew toys.

2.   Begin the game by using your hands much like paws and tapping them gently on your pup's toes.

3.   After a while, try doing the same with your feet as you're lying down on the ground in front of your pup.

4.   Next, stand up and tap your pup's paws with your feet, being careful not to exert too

much pressure. That is, don't step right down on his paws. Turn it into a game of foot dodge so your pup learns to yield to your feet.

Mix this game up with the above advanced umbilical to get your pup dialed in to you and also when you're hanging out at home on rainy days. You can also play this game while you do housework or outdoor chores, such as raking grass and leaves. A broom works as an ideal substitute for your feet because it will brush up against your pup's paws without hurting them, so you can try out this adaptation while you're sweeping the floor. As you continue playing the game, you can use the vacuum cleaner hose (if you're vacuuming) and light furniture that you might be moving around the room. (Don't try it with heavy furniture, of course!) The goal is to acclimatize your pup to yielding to any objects under your control.

Ramp the game up as your pup grows and matures by increasing your speed and the strength you use to tap your pup's paws. (Of course, never hurt his paws in the process!) If your pup learns to yield to your authority in this game, he'll be prepared to move on to fun activities that you can do together like biking and Rollerblading. Remember that the goal is for your pup to have the opportunity to participate in all sorts of different experiences and new activities, and to do that you need to teach him the rules of engagement. Most important, you need to teach him that you're always in the lead, dictating movement, and that he needs to respect that authority.

Talk-to-the-Paws Puppy Yoga

When a puppy gets a lot of outdoor activity, she'll need to take breaks every so often, so she can have a drink or stretch. The best time to do this is in the middle of an outdoor romp and again at the end because she'll be tired after burning off a lot of energy. Break time also gives you a perfect opportunity to do a puppy yoga session, and while you're at it, you can check your pup's coat and between her toes for burrs, insects, sticks, stones or debris. You can also monitor her breathing to make sure she isn't coming close to a heat stroke.

Here's how to do Talk-to-the-Paws Puppy Yoga:

1. Start off the yoga session with a little massage. That is, while your pup is standing, kneel down in front of her and start with a chest rub.

2. And now for the "yoga" part. Stretch one of your pup's front legs forward and massage it slowly and gently. Start with the pressure you'd use to squeeze an avocado and then increase the pressure, working downward to the paw.

3. If your pup's eyelids begin to droop, this is a good thing!

4. Hold on to her paw and slowly and gently pull the limb toward you as you continue massaging her leg.

5. Now stretch the leg upward, gently and gradually pulling until your pup's head and shoulders are raised.

6. Go through Steps 2 to 5 with your pup's other front leg.

7. Then switch to her hind legs, positioning yourself behind and square to your pup. Massage and stretch one of her hind legs in the same way that you massaged her front legs.

8. Go through Steps 2 to 5 with your pup's other hind leg.

Give your pup a stretching massage like this after any strenuous outdoor romps.

Barking at the Moon and Other Obsessive Behaviours

Canines are tuned in to so many things that we can't smell, see or hear. I notice this often around dogs and the full moon. I'll leave the explanation to the scientific experts, but dogs do seem to be affected by the moon in this phase. Many of my clients, for instance, complain about doggy misbehaviours happening at this time of the month. Some house-trained dogs will leave a big brown gift on the carpet—only during a full moon. Other trained dogs will act out during a full moon by flipping you the paw when you ask them to do anything. Or they'll suddenly become a whiny, whimpering or barking gong show come bedtime. If your pup or mature dog suddenly turns moody or rude, check the sky for a full moon. I'm not saying you should give your pup a free pass to trash the joint once a month. Do continue to interrupt and correct any negative behaviours, and consider doing umbilical for two days during the full moon. But keep in mind that your pooch's behaviour might be unusual at this time.

Of course, pups will also react to lightning and thunderstorms by hiding under the bed and cowering. Don't be tempted to overcompensate by coddling your pup or letting him sleep in your bed. Remember, they're not human kids. If you change your attitude now, you'll start sending your pup mixed messages. But you can curb your dog's fear during a storm by closing the curtains or hanging out in the basement or laundry room or another darkened spot in your home.

Sometimes dogs also freak out over the simplest things, like seeing a broom or a vacuum cleaner. For herding dogs, their herding instinct often kicks in when the broom or mop goes into action. Rudy the Schnoodle still goes ape when his archrival, the pushy, noisy vacuum cleaner, suddenly appears out of the closet and rudely sucks all the good, smelly things off the floor. He'll chase that thing around, yapping at it and trying to dominate it, even though it could probably suck him right up like a big ball of lint. But Rudy must think he wins every time because after fifteen minutes the vacuum cleaner goes silent (thus appearing to wave the surrender flag) and skulks its way back into the closet to hatch a plan for the next invasion.

Dogs will react to things that are loud and foreign objects that move. Some common ones include lawn mowers, chainsaws, bikes, strollers, umbrellas (and even canes), walkers and wheelchairs. Remember that dogs have sensitive ears and that they judge anything that moves by body language. So anything that moves very fast or very slow or in a way that's unnatural to canines could trip their doggy alarms. Ditto for things that suddenly morph from one shape to another, like an umbrella.

Such reactions are no big deal, especially if your pup is encountering a specific foreign object for the first time. Your puppy will become familiarized gradually, as long as you're providing him with tons of mental and physical stimulation and exposing him to as many new things as possible. If you don't, he'll likely develop phobias and fixations that will make him unbalanced and could lead to territorial aggression or extreme anxiety. If your pup starts to obsess over anything, say, "Leave it" in a firm tone. And take your pup outside to meet his true doggy needs.

STAGE 7
off-leash puppy power

By the time they're about six months old, puppies will start to shed some of their puppy-ness. They'll start to look more like dogs: their button noses will become snouts and their coats will start to lose that puppy fluffiness. Adding insult to injury, during the five- to seven-month stage of your pup's life, these physical changes tend to overlap with people losing interest in the pup. The novelty and shine will wear off a bit just as puppies' unique personalities are taking form and they start craving new experiences. It's no wonder that canine behavioural attitudes begin to emerge at this stage, but you ain't seen nothing yet! Your pup is nearing the terrible twos phase, so it's imperative that you focus even more on him now. You have only a two-month window of opportunity with your puppy before he starts flipping you the paw!

Leaving the Leash Behind

Think of off-leash training in terms of getting your driver's licence. First you have to study, write a test and get your learner's licence. Then you have to start taking driving lessons and practising in the real world with patient teachers. If your pup doesn't listen to your instructions and doesn't respond to any urgent requests right away while off-leash, it's like running a red light. In that case she should get a "ticket from the cop." She has to be held accountable for breaking the law.

All dogs, no matter what breed or size, should have the right to be off-leash. This is especially critical for herding, hunting and sporting dogs that like to chase down critters. And let's never forget that featherweights and smaller, so-called "toy dogs" also need to run, romp, prance and dance. They shouldn't be stuck in tiny apartments just because they've been pitched as ideal urban lap dogs.

Please don't deny your pup her canine rights and force her to be a wallflower at the dance. Start taking the lead by having the courage to drop that leash. As a confident and fun caregiver, allow your pup to have the opportunity to show you he can be responsible and self-assured.

Off-Leash Training: Phase One

Before you start "formal" off-leash training, it's a good idea to expose your pup gradually to this new mode of being by dropping that leash every so often at dog parks and in other safe outdoor settings. But

DON'T TIE ME DOWN!

I still meet far too many people with adult dogs who say they wouldn't dare allow their dogs to go off-leash. Well, of course, you can't just chuck the leash one day and say, "Go at 'er, dog!" You need to train him to earn that responsibility. But if we lower the bar on expectations about what a puppy can do, we limit the pup's potential. And here's an example of what pups can potentially do. I've started off-leash training many pups at five or six months old, and they were all off-leash-trained by the age of ten months.

Let's be clear: we prevent canines from living at full capacity because of our own ideas, limitations, insecurities, phobias, stubbornness and even laziness. We look at pups as fragile babies, not canines.

But canines go through a rapid developmental process. Babies take days or weeks to learn how to do a simple roll onto their bellies, and they tend to get stuck and need our assistance at first. By comparison, pups learn at an exponential rate. Pups are whiz kids. They're constantly saying, "I need more from this thing called life. I don't want to be a tethered dodge ball! I want to run and dance and sing." Canines will eventually go stir-crazy if they're always confined to your side. Let them develop their full potential. Don't tie them down!

when your pup is about five–seven months old, it's time to ramp it up. First, take your dog on a romp to burn off some steam, pick up the daily news and mix with other dogs. Then find an enclosed outdoor spot like a tennis or basketball court. You can also start this training in your backyard, but you'll eventually need to graduate to more public spaces where there are more distractions. That way you'll be able to accurately gauge your pup's skill sets, as well as your own self-assurance. Remember that pups are sponges dialed in to our energy levels, so if you're nervous, impatient or even distracted, your pup will feel those negative vibes too.

1. Start by walking your pup on-leash. Is he yanking at the leash? If so, do a leash correction (as described in Stage 6) to get him focused on you.

2. Continue walking on-leash until the leash is relaxed.

3. Refrain from chit-chatting at your dog. He doesn't need small talk about the weather or gossip about the neighbours. Let the movement speak for itself. As mentioned before, this will help make your words count when you start directing your pup to sit.

4. Stop and direct your pup to "Stop," enunciating the "P" clearly. Your pup should be able to stop on a dime. If so, praise him with a chest scrunch. If he doesn't stop, do a leash correction and repeat the exercise.

5. Repeat the Stop exercise a few times until your pup is consistently stopping on a dime. Be sure to reward each success with a chest scrunch, and for longer sessions, break for a brief game of tug or fetch with your pup's favourite toy.

6. Take the handle of the leash, and with your arm positioned at your side in an L-shape, with your upper arm tucked close to your core, drape the leash over your hand where the thumb meets your hand. (Your hand should be held out in a gun shape, but with all of your fingers pointing forward.)

7. Continue walking with the leash draped over your hand. If the leash starts to slip, clamp down on it with your thumb, do a quick leash correction, direct your pup to sit and then get the leash back into draped position. Repeat the above process every time the leash slips, being mindful of your movement and the position of your arm. Does your arm start wandering sideways or upward? Bring it back to position. Pretend your holding a ball against your side with your upper arm

8. Increase your pace by 10 percent.

9. If you show any hesitations, inconsistencies or unnatural movements (such as shuffling and wavering), your pup will start to feel the need to take charge. Don't let that happen. Maintain good posture and a confident stride.

10. Keep working on this exercise until there's no strain on the leash and it doesn't slip and your dog is following your lead all the time.

Off-Leash Training:
Phase 2, The Chase Game

Now you're going to add the "Hustle" directive and throw a chase game into the mix.

1. Keep your pup leashed, but put a large, loose knot on the handle end of the leash, so if you need to step on the leash later, the knot will give you extra control.

2. Stand facing your pup square on and direct him to stay.

3. After your pup has been in a stay for one minute, drop the leash and back up about five feet (about one and a half metres) and in an upbeat tone, say, "Hustle."

4. Then turn and jog away from your pup so he chases after you.

5. When he catches up, change directions and continue with the chase game a few times, changing directions a number of times.

6. After a few minutes of playing the chase game, crouch down, open your arms and say, "Hustle." When your pup comes rushing to you, give him a good chest scrunch and play with him for a while.

    The goal is for your pup to chase you continually. If he's not chasing after you, it's a good clue that your pup thinks you're a snoozefest. In that case you'll need to step up your energy and your liveliness. Play some tug or retrieve games and tussle around with your pup. Get into it. Otherwise you'll be failing your pup. You'll be limiting your pup's potential to go off-leash.

7. Now, start from the top with the exercise, but this time, step back a total of ten feet (three metres).

8. Continue with the exercise, increasing the distance between you until there's a twenty-foot (six-metre) distance between you and your pooch.

This process could take days or weeks or months. Be patient and be sure to have fun, mixing the training with playing games and outdoor romps.

Off-Leash Training: Phase 3, Dog Park Tango

For the next stage of training, you'll be satisfying your pup's need for canine socialization by practising off-leash training at the dog park.

1. Start on-leash, holding the leash, but once you assess the goings-on among the canines and humans and decide it's a good time to

THE CANINE COMFORT ZONE

FYI, I didn't come up with the maximum of twenty feet (six metres) in "Off-Leash Training: Phase 3" just by chance. Canines typically have two different comfort zones: one zone is right beside you, and the longer-range comfort zone is between eighteen and twenty-three feet (between five and a half and seven metres), depending on the pup. So if you find your pup starts to get antsy just before you reach twenty feet (six metres), make eighteen feet (five and a half metres) the maximum distance. But if your dog gets upset when you're even closer than that, he'll need more training to increase the length of that comfort zone. (Also see the "Advanced Patience Training" section later in this chapter.)

do so, drop the leash and let your pup play with the other dogs for a while.

2. Back up at least ten feet (three metres), crouch down, open your arms and say, "Hustle." If she hustles, awesome! Give her a chest scrunch.

3. If she doesn't hustle and instead ignores you, don't repeat the verbal directive. Let your pup play for another five minutes and then repeat the Hustle step (Step 2, above).

If she still doesn't run to you this time, don't fret. Be honest with yourself. Did you slack on the basic training, playing and bonding you've read about in the previous chapters? Have you been neglecting your pup's need for outdoor physical and mental exercise? Look at this lack of communication as a take-home lesson and ramp up your leadership and bonding time. If your pup refuses your directive twice, get over there, pick up the leash and take her for a good, long walk.

4. If your pup is dialed in to you and has responded to your direction, she's earned an extra reward.

5. Take off your pup's collar so she's completely unleashed, pat her on the side and give her a gentle push so she knows she can go back to playing with other dogs. Allowing your pup this privilege is the ultimate way to let her speak her own language at full speed, without interpreters, translators and a gaggle of Two Legs who know only the basic phrases of dogspeak: hello, goodbye, bathroom? and thank you.

After a few off-leash sessions in the dog park, where you'll be watching your pup romping with her friends, you'll have a much better understanding of her personality. Maybe she's a party animal or perhaps she prefers hanging one-on-one. Does she like to hang back and watch? Or does she prefer hanging with humans? The possibilities are endless! Embrace every opportunity to let your pup's budding personality shine.

Off-Leash Training:
Phase 4, On the Streets

To be ready for off-leash street training, you'll need to have done the street safety training I described in Stage 5. Off-leash street training is the ultimate test for educating and safeguarding your pup on the streets. And it's the ideal method for tapping into your pup's street smarts and assessing the ways he fits into the rhythm and pulse of the human world. Work through this phase of training in a quiet neighbourhood with long-distance sightlines, so you have plenty of time to notice and deal with any approaching traffic.

1. Start on-leash and practise sit-stay at three or four different curbs, on quiet streets with minimal traffic at intersections. There should be no tension on the leash.

2. Be sure to always position yourself between your pup and the street. At intersections position yourself between your pup and the busiest street going into the intersection.

3. About midway down the street, let the leash drop. Your pup should be following right beside you.

4. Approaching the curb, stop and direct your pup to stop.

5. Now start crossing the street together. In order to communicate a sense of urgency and get

your pup focused, quicken your pace for the first three steps as you move from the curb to the street. Then slow down in the middle of the street as you assess whether any vehicles might be turning at the intersection. Finally, quicken your pace again as you approach the opposite curb.

6. Practise this exercise at least six times and change your pace, but remember to always maintain an assured stride and good posture.

7. To wrap up the session, reward yourself and your dog with a good outdoor romp and some play with you and with other dogs.

Once you've introduced off-leash street training to your pup, work on the exercise daily—while you run errands, on your way to a café and when you go out for walks. Even after your pup has mastered these off-leash skills, do the exercise with the leash in your pocket for a few weeks just to be sure.

As you continue with off-leash training, allow a slightly wider berth between you and your pup. When you do this, your pup might start to dilly-dally over the daily news, which is fine and expected, as long as he responds immediately to any of your verbal or non-verbal cues to "Hustle" or "Stop." Gradually expose your pup to neighbourhoods with higher levels of traffic until you can cruise the city streets with your pup off-leash. That could take weeks or months, depending on his growing skill sets, personality and maturity level. And it will take some time for *you* to become comfortable with and trusting of your pup's smarts. But don't limit his need to explore the world off-leash. Trust is a two-way street.

The Puppy Midterm:
Testing Your Puppy Magnetism

By the time your pup reaches the age of seven months, you should have a great sense of his blossoming personality. But what do you know about your pup's thoughts in relation to you? By now, I hope he will know that you're a patient, consistent, kind, well-balanced and considerate caregiver who meets all of his essential canine needs. But you should also be a fun-loving, upbeat and pleasurable Two Legs to hang with. If you're as dull as ditchwater, a wet blanket, a negative nelly or any other potentially alienating sort of caregiver, you're going to have even more trouble bonding with your pup and training him once he hits the terrible twos.

So act preventively and determine your puppy friendliness with this simple test. Do the test while your pup is off-leash at the dog park, romping around with other canines. If your pup has yet to master off-leash skills, do the game at a fenced-in dog park or invite some dogs over to your place.

1. Let your pup play and socialize with other pups for at least fifteen minutes—longer if he's missed a day or two of socialization time. Stay about eighteen feet (five and a half metres) away from the action. (As I

mentioned earlier, a twenty-foot [six-metre] distance between you and your pup is the typical canine comfort zone.)

2. Note whether or not your pup glances over at you periodically. He should be fully engaged in play, but hopefully he'll do a check-in now and then, monitoring where you are. (If your pup loses it as soon as you're out of eyeball range, refer to the patience training in the next section.)

3. Now go and hide behind a nearby tree or some other object that provides full cover.

4. Now pop out into the open and look for your pup. Ideally, he should be scanning the area for you. Then, when he sees you, he should get all excited and maybe even come ripping over to you. That's the goal! And if this happens, be proud of yourself and your pup because it says so much about your bond. Then keep up the good work by continuing to take that bonding to new heights with lots of play, a good sense of humour and continued dedication to your pup's canine needs.

5. If you find that your pup is still playing with other dogs and doesn't even notice that you've been out of sight, from your pup's viewpoint, it means that you've either been neglecting his canine needs for exercise,

stimulation and socialization or he thinks you're dreadfully dull—or both. This happens with many of my clients, and they're often really shocked and hurt to find out that their dog views them in this gloomy, negative way. But this huge eye opener can actually be a catalyst for ramping up the fun factor. Raising a pup is serious business, but for training and bonding to be effective, you need to be engaging and attractive to your pup.

If your pup didn't respond to this game and you've just discovered that he considers you a bore, play more on-the-ground games with him daily—like tug and wrestling. Put more physicality into your tussling and romping with your pup. It never ceases to inspire me when I see the way a pup or dog reacts to human playfulness. I often engage in play with a pup or dog to break the ice—tussling around, doing somersaults, jumping around, even digging in the snow or the sand. No matter what the dog owners have said in advance about the dog's alleged issues, that initial playfulness always immediately dials a dog in to focusing on me. The humans are usually gape-mouthed and shocked to see a grown man cavorting around on the grass or the carpet, but the canine always responds positively. Remember that the number one priority is getting your puppy engaged with you and harnessing that bundle of energy, curiosity and smarts.

Separation Anxiety

Canines develop separation anxiety for a variety of reasons. Some puppies acquire it if they've been removed from their litter before the age of eight weeks. Many develop separation anxiety because they've been left alone far too much and their canine needs for outdoor exercise, mental stimulation and lots of dog-to-dog socializing have been neglected. Others aren't left alone enough, so they've never built up the confidence to fly solo. And then there are the dogs with anxiety issues who are overcoddled and smothered by caregivers who are oblivious to the importance of providing a balanced, canine-friendly life.

A perfect storm occurs when all of the above negative human behaviours are heaped on one puppy or dog. Sadly, I've met and trained many of these canines and their owners—and both are very hard to fix and steer onto a positive path. This is especially true of mature dogs, who tend to develop side-effect issues: excessive barking, fearfulness around other people and dogs, depression, obsessive compulsive behaviour and potentially dangerous dominance and aggressive behaviours.

People are often clueless about the part that their own behaviours and attitudes play in creating these anxiety-related negative traits. But here's a checklist that will help you diagnose whether your pup or mature dog has these issues:

Signs of Separation Anxiety
- When you leave home or even, in some cases, when you're out of direct eyeball range, your pup

barks non-stop; shivers and shakes uncontrollably; trashes your possessions (or chews or licks things obsessively); scratches at the doors, windows or floors; or engages in any other unruly behaviours all the time.

- Your pup exhibits overt insecurity and fearfulness around other dogs that appears aggressive (such as lashing out, baring teeth or growling deeply) or uses body language that appears unnecessarily overprotective (such as a lowered head combined with a compressed neck). Some pups with separation anxiety will even urinate whenever a human hand approaches or when they're touched.

- Your pup appears overly shy around people and other dogs and cowers near your legs, hides under tables and beds, or bolts whenever someone approaches.

- Your pup often exhibits hangdog body language: slumped shoulders and head, a shuffling gait, a tail constantly between the legs and an overall appearance of self-consciousness and even depression.

Anxious Hangdogs

Researchers have found that dogs with separation anxiety are more likely to have elimination issues and destructive tendencies and to act excessively stressed out when their owners leave and return home.[19] Studies have also found that the *owners* of anxious dogs were 2.5 times more likely to be single people[20] and tended to provide only verbal discipline for misbehaviour.[21]

Human Habits That
Increase Puppy Anxieties

Here's another assessment method, but this one focuses on the human behaviours and actions that typically accompany canine separation anxiety. Be honest with your self-diagnosis and stop doing these things immediately. Break these habits and release your pup from the grip of low self-esteem and anxiety. (Note that these problems also apply to mature, anxious dogs.)

- You neglect your pup's basic canine needs by tolerating household unruliness and failing to hold him accountable with disciplinary measures.

- You allow your pup to dominate you by giving him free rein with the human furniture (especially your bed) and by allowing him to jump up on furniture and people.

- You engage in long, emotionally wrought hellos and goodbyes and treat any separation as a Greek tragedy.

- You reward and even nurture your pup's insecurities, anxieties and even aggressive behaviours by giving him treats; picking him up off the ground; engaging in lots of repetitive chatter; overcoddling him with human affection (especially excessive hugs and kisses and petting him a lot while he sits on your lap); limiting or isolating your pet

from socializing with other dogs so that your pup
has little or no opportunity to learn the canine
rules of conduct from other dogs; and showering
your pup with a multitude of toys and clothes.

- You tend to isolate yourself from other people and
  animals and expect your pup to fill all those shoes.

- You haven't learned to harness your pup's innate
  skills during bonding and training by learning to
  speak canine, using confident body language.

Treating Separation Anxiety

Besides *immediately* kicking your own negative
habit(s) (from the ones illustrated above), you will
need to do advanced patience training. I'll walk you
through that in a minute. I also recommend imple-
menting the training regimen in the next chapter: umbilical training combined with no talking. That's an
ideal exercise for people who tend to chatter a lot and
are tempted to coo and verbally coddle their animals.

Most important, you will need to start letting your
pup or dog socialize with other dogs immediately.
Start by setting up a play date with one or two friends
or colleagues who have healthy, well-behaved adult
dogs. Leash the dogs up, but let the leash trail on the
ground, so you can step in if necessary. Otherwise,
leave them to their own devices. As I said earlier, the
canine pack is highly adaptive, and they typically
work out their own system of pack order fairly and
efficiently. But they will sponge up any negative

human energy, so give them space and try to limit your own negative energy levels.

After your pup has been socializing with dogs that you know, start taking your canine to the dog park as soon as possible. (Review Stage 5 again as a refresher.) Do your best not to cramp your dog's canine style, and you'll soon be able to see your animal's true personality bud and blossom.

Advanced Patience Training

Pups and dogs with separation anxiety should never get a free pass for misbehaving. Like any other canines, they need to be held accountable for their antics. Otherwise, they'll never learn to become confident, content members of the domestic pack. My patience-training technique mixes up that accountability factor with acclimatizing a canine to becoming comfortable flying solo. And the focus in that part is on being content to loaf around and snooze away the majority of the day—a necessary state of doggy mind for domestic, homebound dogs with working parents. This exercise could take some time, so give yourself a number of hours before work, or start this training on the weekend. Here's how to do it:

1. When you leave the house, don't make a big show of it. Don't say anything verbal to your pup, and if you have a dog with serious separation anxiety issues, don't even touch him.

2. After you've closed the front door, listen for

any barking or whining. If your pup is protesting, open the front door and say, "No noise" in a firm tone.

3. Re-exit, and if he loses it again, repeat the directive above.

4. Did your pup lose it *again?* Repeat as above until your canine isn't barking as soon as the door closes.

5. Lurk outside for up to ten minutes. If your dog freaks out at any point, consider returning and giving him a leash correction instead of the verbal command. (Especially for those of you who tend to ooververbalize, chances are your pup has become desensitized to *your* barking.)

6. When you return home, don't make a big show of greeting your pup. I recommend keeping it zipped completely and refraining from touching him. If you must, give one chest scrunch and immediately leash up your pup for a good, long outdoor romp.

7. If you've discovered that your pup has trashed something or peed or pooped, you must never ignore it—that only rewards negative behaviours. Say, "Unacceptable" or "Leave it" in a firm tone and consider putting your pup in a fifteen-minute time out. Then get outside for a walk and some socialization.

Don't Cave!

Remain calm while doing this training. The worst thing you can do is show signs of impatience, anger, regret or most especially, guilt. Expect all sorts of manipulative antics from your canine. The more antics, the more confirmation that your pup believes you'll cave in—but don't let that happen. You might need to repeat this regimen many times before your pup becomes comfortable alone, in his own skin.

8. Zip it while you're out walking or romping. Your pup doesn't need to hear about your office drama or what you bought for dinner tonight. (And remember that your pup should be dining on dog food!) Save the human chatter for people you meet en route.

9. Consistency is the key here—like everything else with canine relations.

Hide-and-Seek

Who doesn't love a game of hide-and-seek? Especially on rainy or cold days when you're stuck at home. Puppies and dogs love the game too, and it's one of the top activities I recommend for clients with unruly dogs and alpha dogs because it gets your canine psyched up and focused on your leadership capabilities. (This is much better than your being forced into the position of chasing after your animal all the time, which means that the canine is controlling the movements—a big no-no). For puppies the benefits are obvious: a wired-for-sound pup is always raring to play. But hide-and-seek helps with the patience training, since you're directing your pup to wait and then providing an exciting reward when she finds you. Here's how to do it.

1.   Direct your pup into a sit-stay.

2.   Leave the room and find a hiding spot within earshot, but don't make it tough on your pup—at least not for the first few sessions as she's getting the hang of the game.

3.   Call out, "Hustle" in an upbeat tone.

4.   Your pup might smell you before she sees you. When she finds you, say something upbeat like "Good job. You found me." Then give your pup a chest scrunch.

5.   Repeat the game, but choose a slightly harder-to-find spot or a place that's farther from your sit-staying pup.

6.   Mix up the game with nonverbal "Hustle" commands like clapping and whistling.

7.   If your pup is still getting the hang of sit-staying when you're not within eyeball range, add another person to the mix. Have that person hide while you stay with your pup to make sure she sits and stays. When the hider is ready, you and your pup can play seek together. (Kids love playing this game, and they should be the ones to go and hide. If you have young children with high-pitched voices,

when they're ready to have the pup find them, have them clap their hands instead.)

8. Mix up hide-and-seek games into your outdoor romps and your training exercises as well, so your pup can focus on you among all the distractions of outdoor life.

STAGE 8

the terrible twos: divas, rebels and canine accountability

Pull out a big bag of patience and get ready for some cardio because you're probably going to find yourself chasing after your pup a lot during the seven-ish- to nine-ish-month period of your pup's life. I call this period "the terrible twos" because your pup's behaviour might remind you of the way a toddler starts to bolt away from her parents and beelines for the electrical outlets. It's also a time when you're suddenly going to start to see tantrums, meltdowns and all sorts of manipulative behaviours emerging as your four-legged friend explores the wider world and pushes her boundaries. So now, more than ever, it's important to remain calm, cool, collected, assertive and consistent as leader of the household pack. And remember that this stage won't last forever—only about four weeks.

You're probably thinking that after harping away about the dangers of humanizing dogs, I'm sending you a big old mixed message by comparing puppies at this stage of development to a toddler in the terrible twos. But I've made an exception in this one case because it really helps underline the fact that, like us, dogs are constantly evolving, honing their skills, pushing boundaries and developing their own unique personalities. But please remember that your puppy is a canine, which means that he or she has developed one essential canine skill that human toddlers thankfully haven't (and which has no place in the domestic pack): the ability to hunt and eat prey in order to survive.

By the age of six months, wild dogs have been taught to take down small prey and contribute these resources to the dog pack. Meanwhile, domestic pups in our human packs have spent six months watching us rip open bags of chow, so their hunting skills haven't been harnessed. But—and this is a big but—if pups are allowed or encouraged to assume alpha status at any point during the terrible twos, those canine instincts might just kick in. You'll then have a lot of difficulty later on with dangerous behaviours like stalking and territorial aggression. Please allow me another toddler reference to highlight the puppy view of the world. If a two-year-old has a morning meltdown and demands candy for breakfast, succumbing to that toddler's demands isn't just downright unhealthy; it actually rewards negative behaviours and makes you look weak. It sets a precedent that can be really tough to break tomorrow. And if you saw a parent or guardian continue to feed their toddler candy for breakfast, you'd call that abuse, right?

Whatever you call it in the human world, in the canine world, I think it's abusive to submit to a pup's demands, antics and attempts to dictate the household rules. So I implore you to embrace your obligations as your pup's caregiver and leader—especially during this stage of your pup's development. The terrible twos last for about four weeks, and the latter half is usually the worst of it. Suddenly, house-trained pups are pooping all over the place. A pup who could sit-stay for five minutes a few days ago or stop on a dime during off-leash training is flipping you the paw and bolting away at every single opportunity. Or yanking you around on the leash. Or trashing your bed of roses. Or jumping up all over you. Or mooching food from the counters and the table. I've seen one pint-sized pup do all of those things.

This is typically when I come into the picture. I meet a pup who has an entire family of humans wrapped around his paws. I meet an incredibly smart young pooch manipulating all the Two Legs in the pack. And most of the puppy owners who call on me think their pup is the stupid one. Nothing could be farther from the truth! All pups go through the terrible twos because they're *curious* and *smart.* So this is the worst time to lose faith in your pup's abilities! It's also the most dangerous time to neglect your pup's needs by shirking your alpha leader responsibilities or slacking off on meeting the pup's physical, psychological and social needs. Maybe now that the pup has lost some of his cute magnetism, *your* human behaviours have changed. The pup may have been getting too many mixed messages or, worse, sensing disinterest and misbehaving just to grab back some much-needed attention.

This is a crucial period in your pup's life. I recommend not adding any new training to the mix at this point. Instead, it's the ideal time to get back to the basics that I've already covered—especially umbilical training—and I'll be walking you through some important new umbilical techniques in this chapter.

Remember that with a lot of consistency and hard work, this four-week period will pass without too much damage. In fact, once it's over, you'll have a much better understanding of your pup's smarts and personality traits. If you take your time and are extra patient now, there will be a huge payoff by the time your pup is nine months old and the benefits will continue throughout his life.

Phase One: Re-Leash the Puppies!

You'll know your seven- to nine-month-old pup has hit the terrible twos when the inconsistent behaviour starts. Even when it comes to basic training like sit-stay, you'll see your pup cocking her head when you use verbal or snap directives—and you'll notice that her attention span has diminished. If your pup has had a lot of success with initial off-leash training, suddenly she'll no longer respond to your "Hustle" and she'll no longer stop on a dime with a "Stop" directive. Training hits an apparent flatline as your pup gradually seems to become more and more oblivious to your directions.

As soon as you notice these traits emerge, stop any off-leash training immediately. Don't curb the outdoor activities, since your pooch will still need to burn off energy, but do all outdoor walking and dog-to-dog socializing on-leash or in fenced-in dog parks or other secure locations. The goal at this stage is to safeguard your pup from the many potential hazards she'll encounter if she chooses to bolt.

Nearing the end of that first week, many puppy owners will say to me, "Geez, my stellar pup is suddenly brain dead." He isn't! He's just going through a confused period as he pushes the boundaries, and this means you'll need to bring in a cartload of patience, clarity and consistency. You'll need to return to all the basic training techniques I introduced in previous chapters and ramp up your concise, assured body movements and gestures. At the end of the no-talking period that I'll describe in a minute, you'll also need to focus on keeping your verbal directives simple, crystal clear and well-enunciated.

About midway into the second week of the terrible twos, many of my clients will say, "It's not too bad. Not a big deal, Brad." Just you wait until the following week! Meanwhile, as I mentioned earlier, make sure you're not overstimulating your pup's brain with any new training, especially off-leash training. You won't get anywhere with the new skills, and you'll just pile up the frustrations for both species and be tempted to give up. And that's the last thing you should do right now! Get right back to the basics and make sure you're mixing up training sessions with a lot of bonding time and exercising outdoors. Go out on lots of adventurous *on-leash* walks to new places—and ramp up the physical exercise and the dog-to-dog socializing. While you're at home, continue playing tug games and engaging with your pup on the ground.

Phase Two: Monster Pups

All of a sudden, come Week 3, you'll have a Frankenpup on your hands who bolts at every opportunity. Sadly, I've seen too many puppies' lives cut short during the terrible twos, so whatever your pup's past successes with off-leash training, keep that training on the back burner during this four-week period and keep your pup on-leash outdoors. Leash up your pup before you leave home, before you get out of your vehicle and at any unenclosed dog parks. Those of you with backyards should also be extra cautious that your pup hasn't found or created a secret escape hatch. Do a perimeter search of your fence lines to make sure there are no holes. It's not good to leave a pup in the backyard unsupervised for long periods at any time in his life, but be especially careful during the terrible twos.

Behavioural issues also emerge during the monster pup phase. A house-trained pup suddenly starts leaving surprise gifts for you around the house and seems clueless when you get upset about it. He might also start barking at the leaves blowing on the trees and become hypersensitized to sudden movements and sounds. Some pups will start trashing your stuff.

Suddenly, that roll of toilet paper, or whatever item he fixated on in the early weeks, becomes irresistible again. These misbehaviours often have nothing to do with the dog owner shirking responsibilities, but you're going to have to batten down the hatches and make sure you return to the puppy-proofing basics I outlined in Stage 3. That is, you'll have to keep bathroom and bedroom doors closed and make sure that things like garbage cans, electrical wires and human food are stored safely out of reach.

It's also imperative that you don't cave on interrupting, correcting and disciplining misbehaviours. At this stage your pup is going to roll out all his manipulative qualities, and if you habituate your pup to getting away with these tactics, even for this final two-week period of the terrible twos, you'll have many issues moving forward. Instead, micromanage your pup now. (I'll walk you through my interruption and correction techniques in the next several sections of this chapter.)

Zip It Up: Umbilical Training With No Talking

I recommend establishing a no-talking rule while you do umbilical during the final stage of the terrible twos, so you can really get in sync with your pup's body language. Remember that when it comes to communicating with your pup, actions speak louder than words.

Now is the time to ramp up your dogspeak communication skills by initiating a household no-talking

All Action and No Talk

When the terrible twos arrive, you'll be relieved if you've spent the past seven months keeping the human chatter to a minimum. That way your pup will have been spared all that ear-splitting human barking and you'll have had the chance to hone your body language, gestures and action. All of this will make your pup more likely to listen to you, even during these rebellious four weeks.

policy while you do umbilical training. I don't mean that you should never speak to your pup (especially if she still has trouble with nonverbal directions, like snapping, clapping and physical gestures). But I recommend that you keep the chit-chat to a minimum during these four weeks when interacting with your pup. The no-talking rule is especially helpful if you have a tendency to voice any negative feelings such as anxiety, impatience and frustration. It's also a good method for self-control when your pup stresses you out so much that you're tempted to bark angrily, repeating orders like a skipping CD.

If you're in a multi-person household, it would be ideal to apply the no-talking rule to everyone living there as you go through the final two weeks of your pup's terrible twos. Some clients are shocked and dismayed by this idea, and they don't think it will make much difference. But as soon as they zip it, they see huge benefits, not just in relation to their canine's behavioural issues, but also because it harmonizes communication with each other. In dogspeak, doing umbilical during this period heightens the level of body language–based communication and underlines your pup's need to follow your lead at all times because she

has to keep tuned in to your ongoing physical movements, not just your occasional commands.

I recommend doing umbilical for about 20 percent of your time with your pup during this two-
week period and doing some of it outdoors and some
at home. Too much umbilical is a bit like holding a
toddler's hand all the time when she should be
learning to walk on her own. But if you do too little
umbilical, you won't be providing your pup with
enough of the safety he needs while he's going
through this stage of bolting at every opportunity.
Remember too, that the umbilical technique loses its
power to harness your pup's attention if the sessions
are too brief.

The No-Talking Playbook

Here are some point-form tips for navigating the
no-talking period and maximizing the benefits. The
goal is to tap into all of the tools in the training toolbox that I've already introduced you to. Remember
that the key to efficacy is to *show* your dog what you
want with concise, crystal-clear movement. And try
to zip it for two weeks, at least while you are within
earshot of your puppy. I bet that within the first hour,
your pup will be looking up at you, wondering if a
cat got your tongue. As I've said many times before,
the key is to get your pup to focus on you.

- Be wary if your pup tries to manipulate you into
  speaking by pulling out the big doe eyes or even
  barking to bait you into a long-winded debate. If

she barks, it simply means that you've been talking to your pup too much and she's become used to this method of getting your attention. Don't ignore your canine's needs, but don't habituate your dog to scoring wins on unhealthy behaviours. Within four days at the most, she'll understand that silence is golden.

- During any basic sit-stay training, replace verbal directives with snap, clap or hand gesture direction.

- If you can't get your dog to sit with a nonverbal command, do a leash-guided sit: draw up on the leash so it acts like a teeter-totter, making your pup's head tilt upward and his backside downward.

- Don't slack on allowing your pup to socialize with other dogs, but limit yourselves to enclosed dog parks for off-leash sessions, and keep your pup leashed with the leash trailing. When you need to leave the park, don't use the "Hustle" or "Come" directive. Instead, crouch down, clap your thighs and then open your arms. If your pup flips you the paw, go over to him, pick up the leash and guide him away.

- When you want your pup to chill or go to bed, walk him on-leash to his bed and point to it. If your pup refuses to go to bed on his own steam, do a leash correction and guide him right onto the bed. Then do a "Stop" gesture with your hand, just as you would with Stop training. If your pup continues to flip you the paw, grab his collar and guide him back to the chill zone.

- Before you leave home with your pup, leash him up or put him on umbilical.

- When you return home, tie the leash to the knob of the front door until you've removed your coat and shoes.

- If you need to get your pup's attention at any point, use a whistle or any nonverbal command.

If your pup misbehaves—jumping up on people or on any human furniture, barking excessively, trashing your stuff or eliminating indoors—be sure to interrupt him and correct any house-rule fouls. Once you wrap up the two-week no-talking policy, you'll notice that your verbal directions have a huge extra impact on your puppy. This beautifully illustrates how important the element of surprise is for canines.

Holding Your Canine Accountable

The goal is to use any physical corrections sparingly and only when they're justifiable. As with everything else in dogspeak, if you do too little or too much, your pup won't get the message that you're a consistent, trustworthy leader of his pack. Remember that these techniques are not about brute physical force; they're about speed, agility, balance and consistency.

DOG TANTRUMS:
DR. JEKYLL AND MR. HYDE

Expect many meltdowns and puppy tantrums during the four-week period of the terrible twos, no matter how well the training has gone so far. All pups—no matter how sweet and obedient they used to be—are going to put you through the paces, pushing the envelope and testing whether you'll tolerate these eruptions. For some pups, the tantrums are in-your-face and overt, like home wrecking or growling in a territorial way during tug games or around other dogs and people. Many puppies learn to manipulate in such a crafty, passive-aggressive way that you might not even know they're doing it, but they're actually hoodwinking you! I love it! Again, it shows me a pup's unique smarts and personality. They accelerate these behaviours especially when they know they've done something wrong and they want to distract you from correcting the unruliness. Every time you ignore these games and controlling antics, your pup scores a very unhealthy win, so consider each meltdown an opportunity to glimpse your pup's personality blossoming in front of you. This is not the time to get angry and impatient and stressed, but be sure to hold your pup accountable for her misbehaviours.

They're about maintaining a mutual level of respect and understanding. That way your puppy can adapt to the rules of the interspecies pack and become a healthy, well-balanced, productive member of that pack. Unlike misguided methods like treat training, shock collars, shock fences and other sonic devices, my correction techniques are additional tools in a big toolbox packed with positive training and bonding methods. In puppy training, they're meant to be used sparingly only after the many other tools I've discussed in previous chapters have been used to lay the foundation. As I've said before, canines use physical discipline to underline the urgency of following the rules of conduct in the canine world because the survival of the pack depends on it.

Interruption and Correction Techniques

In the next several sections, I'll be giving you a number of different tools for your interruption and correction toolbox. You might have to try out a few before you can identify the most effective ones for your pup in specific scenarios. I've already discussed dealing with training-related fouls with a leash-guided correction, but that's not a disciplinary action; it's a method for focusing canine attention and motivation. I'm a firm believer that dogs should not be disciplined for any training-related challenges. So please be sure that you do *not* use any of the following corrections in any training situation. These techniques are meant for specific canine misbehaviours that require discipline.

Jumping Up

Puppies start jumping up at a very young age, starting from when they're attempting to get food from their canine moms or wrestling around with their mom and siblings. If the pup has already been fed and continues to leap up at her mom or gets too pushy and aggressive with play, the mom will correct her by growling deeply from the lower part of her chest, to show she means business. She might also show her teeth or curl her lip, and if that doesn't stop the pup from jumping up, she'll give her a quick nip or peck or even pin the pup to the ground with her body and teeth. As puppies mature, if they continue to attempt to dominate by jumping up or mounting, pack leaders, elder dogs and more dominant dogs will ramp up their level of physicality as they discipline the pup. That's because the last thing a well-balanced dog pack needs is some muscle-head lug making trouble.

Ditto in the human world. In dogspeak, jumping up is a form of domination. Because the canines in the pack need to cooperate, not dominate, pack leaders will discipline dominating actions swiftly and effectively. These disciplines are not vindictive actions wrought by an evil pack leader hell-bent on world domination. They're carried out by balanced leaders to restore health and balance to the pack. Sometimes the pack leaders are a pair of parents. Sometimes it's an elder—an experienced dog in the pack—and when that elder grows old or dies, someone else has to fill his or her role.

In the domestic human pack, if you allow a dog to jump up, you're sending a mixed message that your pup has no choice but to interpret as a crack in your leadership capabilities or a job offer for him (the pup) to herd or keep watch. With domestic dogs, each successful jump up weakens your position.

Perhaps you've had tons of success in staving off this bad habit—until the terrible twos—and now your pup is suddenly attempting to overthrow you from the comfy lounge chair and the bed. She might also be trying to take your place at the head of the table by mooching around, hovering for food under the table and trying to steal food from counters. It might not seem like a big deal now, but the jumping up often accelerates into more aggressive behaviours like nipping, pouncing, biting into clothing to herd peoples' movement and, of course, more serious biting. A good number of my clients have nearly given up their pups because of these serious behavioural issues. Don't let it go there. Step up to your leadership position and interrupt the jumping up. In the next two sections, I'll describe two techniques for doing this.

The Peck Fake-Out

This is for pups who jump up on or toward furniture or people. As soon as your pup starts to rear up (or in some cases, your pup might growl, bark or even nip at your foot or pant leg just prior to moving), you'll need to act fast with this physical technique. It will spell out the crystal-clear message "Don't even think about it."

1. Dart your hand down toward your pup's face, neck or side at a forty-five-degree angle to fake a dog peck, but withdraw your hand as quickly as possible. Your hand should not contact your pup. This move is a bit like the flop that athletes do, like hockey or

basketball players pretending they've been hit to get a foul call even though there was no physical contact.

2. Do this move *every single time* your pup attempts to jump up.

3. If the interruption doesn't work, you're probably not putting enough speed and brevity into the movement. Increase the speed of each fake peck until it becomes one fluid movement. (But never practise this move on your dog when she's *not* engaging in any negative behaviours.)

The Hand Throw Down

This is another method that tells your pup, "Don't get any ideas," if he jumps up toward you after a greeting or if he tries to mooch food from the dinner table or counter.

1. Move your hand down fast, palm angled toward your pup's face. Your hand should come within one-sixteenth of an inch (about a millimetre) of your pup's face, and it might even tickle his eyebrows. But if your pup continues to jump, your pup's snout might run into your hand. That's fine. He needs to learn to heed to your movements, not the other way around.

2. If you're sitting at the table and have a large-breed pup, you may have to stand up to make this interruption count. Do this move *every single time* your pup attempts to jump up. If you allow jumping up when you're wearing sweat pants but not when you're dressed up for work or a night out, you're sending your pup mixed messages. Canines can't tell the difference between a pair of grubby jeans and a three-thousand-dollar suit. Ditto for encouraging jumping up on you but expecting your pup to know that this isn't acceptable behaviour with teeny-tiny toddlers. As usual, be consistent, and don't let a pup jump up on anyone.

Excessive Barking: I'm Shouting Because I'm Sad

This is another behaviour that may not have been an issue until the terrible twos. Some pups are chattier than others and many dogs will bark excessively, but typically only when they've been sitting around the house all day listening for the sound of the garage door or the key in the lock. Then, when all the Two-Legs show up and still don't meet their pup's needs, it's no wonder their dogs will often start barking. Basically, they're saying, "Hey, what about me? I need a walk. I need to play tug. I need to socialize. I need to tell you how I scared off the squirrels, the birds and the postie, *again*."

I'm always amazed at how little tolerance humans have for a little reunion barking from their dogs, especially after they've been gone for nine hours and the dog has had nothing interesting to put in her daytimer. Yet now that she's psyched to see her pack members, all she gets is a bunch of rude human barking, telling her to be quiet. By this time, the level of miscommunication has scaled up into a ridiculous shouting contest: nobody is listening to anyone. That's why my no-talking policy is so essential, especially if you and/or your pup have had a long, hard day at the office.

Many barking dogs have developed territorial issues. Remember that dogs, like people, need to have a purpose in life, and dogs that are forced into self-employment create jobs for themselves to "earn their keep." Many canines of all breeds are attracted to watchdog jobs, from the featherweight mini-cops to the big, burly Rotties that look like bad cops but are typically total pussycats. Pups that are bored out of their skulls can easily get used to barking at every bee that flies by the window. Dogs will use their noggins to be creative and fend off anxiety or boredom, so singing a song (barking) is simply another method of stimulation.

Of course, intense, noisy barking is unacceptable and it shouldn't be allowed. But remember that neither should excessive human barking. Instead of ramping up the verbal diarrhea, try the following technique. But remember to first give your pup the opportunity to give you a few brief headlines from her daily news, and be sure to meet your pup's need for exercise and socialization.

Interrupting the Bark Song

1. Once your pup starts barking, acknowledge your pup by saying, "Okay, [insert pup's name]."

2. If the barking continues, in a firm tone, say, "Leave it." Your tone should be a bit like a parent's tone with noisy kids, sounding that first warning to pipe down. It should be firm and deep but not hostile.

3. If your pup continues barking, you'll need to strengthen the tone in your voice when you say a firm "No noise." It will be a bit like a parent saying, "Enough fooling around" or the ever popular, "Don't make me come up there."

4. Never use a high-pitched voice to interrupt your barking pup. As I've said earlier, canines interpret this as pain and weakness, so that will just make your pup bark even harder, thinking she has to be protective.

5. If your pup continues barking, try a leash correction if she's on-leash or on umbilical.

6. During the two-week no-talking period, let that leash speak for you to intensify your pup's focus. You could also consider one of the disciplinary methods I'll discuss in the next section or the "Advanced Patience Training" in Stage 7.

Home-Wrecking Hounds:
Chewing, Digging and Trashing

Even a stellar pup might start trashing the joint during the terrible twos. As with the jumping up and excessive barking, he'll do this to ward off boredom and stimulate himself because he's becoming more curious and testing the boundaries of his world. In the domestic sphere, some pups will craft a song; others will treat the leather couch like tasty prey and feel pretty good about themselves for poaching such big game. Enter irate Two Legs and that pup will be utterly confused about why his owner is so upset. He won't understand that you spent an entire pay-cheque on that piece of furniture. Ditto for pups who've spent the entire day digging in the potted plants for vermin.

Of course, you shouldn't tolerate home wreck-ing, but you need to understand why pups do these things. Again, a pup who behaves in these ways during the terrible twos is not being vindictive. However, if you cave on your responsibility to use these antics as teaching moments, your pup could easily graduate to habitual home wrecking. Hold your pup accountable.

Here's what to do:

1.   Take your pup to the scene of the crime.

2.   Point to the trashed item and say, "Unac-ceptable" in a firm, deep tone. (As usual, it doesn't matter exactly what words or phrase you use. But say something simple and easily

enunciated. Remember not to use "Stop" because that word should be reserved for off-leash commands.)

3. Put your pup on umbilical so he doesn't have free rein with the house.

4. For repeated or more serious home wrecking, put your pup in a timeout (as described in the section immediately below).

5. If you catch your pup in the act of trashing, say, "Leave it" in a firm, deep tone.

6. If possible, take the wrecked object away from your pup.

Doggy Correction: The Timeout

The timeout is a highly effective method of correcting and disciplining dogs that I've adapted from observing wolf and other canine packs. As with the above methods of interruption and correction, the timeout isn't about physical force or brute dominance; it's about psychology. The key is isolation. Think about it. The threat of being sent out of the pack in the animal kingdom is serious business: it means loss of safety, companionship and survival resources.

I've seen wolves and domestic dogs lead an unruly pup or dog away from the pack and isolate him in a spot just beyond the action for a period of time. For your domestic pup, here's how to do it:

1. After you've said whatever words you use to reprimand your pup verbally once, don't say anything else. Keep your mouth zipped.

2. Leash up your pup and guide him to a spot with a door, a banister or some other fixed object that's just at the periphery of the human action but still within your sightline. Then tie him to it.

3. The goal is to isolate your pup and limit his freedom of movement and engagement for a period of time. He'll be able to see you and all the goings-on, but he won't be able to participate in the mix. And because you can see him, you'll be able to monitor his behaviour periodically.

Keep your pup in the timeout for about fifteen minutes or longer, depending on the nature of the misbehaviour. Once you bring your pup back into the human pack, he may be so happy to be part of the action again that he'll stop his destructive behaviour in order to stay. If he continues or resumes his misbehaviour, put him in another timeout.

As I've mentioned earlier, many dog-training methods are inhumane, even if they're aggressively marketed as positive. Because my methods are based on the behaviour of canine packs, they're effective without being destructive to your pet's well-being. In fact, after seven months of incorporating my positive methods of training and bonding into your life with your puppy, you will have made great strides in your relationship and built a strong foundation for your future together. But in order to maintain those gains, you must correct negative behaviours—during the terrible twos and later on. Your pup has to be held accountable for her actions. That's the only way you'll have a happy and stimulating life together.

STAGE 9

the juvenile period: urban agility training and bonding

We all remember what it was like to be a teenager. It's such a surreal phase. On the one hand, you crave new liberties and freedoms, you want to be with your friends 24/7 and your parents drive you crazy. But you also crave your parents' respect, admiration and trust. You know that you still need them a heck of a lot—not just to feed and shelter you, but also to safeguard you, even if you, like, totally hate all their insane rules. Well, that is pretty much what your pup is going through from about nine to ten months of age. The puppy cutes are gone, gone, gone, never to return, and while the pup has as much as a year before reaching physical maturity, she will need to be spayed or neutered. That's why, among other things, I'll be discussing the basics of pre-surgery and post-surgery care in this chapter.

Hormones and physical packaging aside, this juvie-like period of your pup's life is fraught with emotional changes. You'll probably notice your pup start to act like a zoned-out space cadet when you ask him to use even basic skills like a thirty-second sit-stay. This means you'll have to work really hard to find new and tantalizing ways to engage your pup's attention and respect. Now that the terrible twos are over, it would be a great idea to start up the off-leash training again. I also recommend introducing urban agility training at this stage, as well as providing loads of socialization with old and new dog and people friends. Take your juvie pooch out for novel experiences and to places that will stimulate him and meet his need for variety.

This period represents a fine balance for pup owners and for pups. While your animal will be craving freedom, he won't be socially or emotionally mature enough to be completely trusted until he proves himself capable. It's a Catch-22 here for pup owners, because you have to trust your pup enough to give him that first taste of freedom, and the ideal way to build his trustworthiness is to have confidence and belief not just in him, but also in yourself. (Again, this is where your body language is so important!)

Your goal will be to establish and maintain mutual trust. You'll need to nurture a win-win relationship that balances your pup's emerging need for freedom and novelty with her need for continued structure and guidance.

Spaying or Neutering:
Before, During and After

There's so much debate around the ideal time to have your pup spayed or neutered. Some say you should spay or neuter as early as eight weeks of age, and many shelter pups are fixed on-site, but otherwise, I recommend having this surgery done after the first heat, which happens at about nine months. Sexual maturity arrives at different times with every dog, and when considering a serious operation like spaying or neutering, you will have to look at your pet's maturity as a whole. What is your dog capable of managing at this point in his life? What is his comfort level with the vet? With being alone? With being around other dogs? Maybe he's picking on dogs at the dog park. Males will have less testosterone after being fixed, so generally speaking, their aggression will decrease post-op. However, all dogs have different levels of aggression in the first place. I know intact male dogs who never pick fights.

One thing is clear: one reason there are so many neglected dogs in the world is that they haven't been spayed or neutered, so now is the time to talk to your vet about having your pup fixed. You'll not only avoid accidental pregnancies; socializing with other dogs will become a much more relaxed experience all around.

- Prior to surgery, make sure that you've discussed pre-operative rules with your vet, like no eating starting the night before surgery.

- Get post-surgical advice from your vet about potential mobility issues for at least a week and even up to two weeks after your pup is fixed.

- For the amount of time your vet suggests, keep your pup leashed during walks and don't let him do any strenuous activities (like running around and jumping up and getting in and out of vehicles). This will prevent the stitches from being pulled or ripped.

- Don't let your pup go swimming, and do not bathe your pup for ten days.

- Check the sutures daily. If they're external, don't worry if the area around the sutures is slightly red and sore looking. But if the area seems to be excessively swollen—and especially if there's leakage or bleeding from the stitches—talk to your vet immediately.

- Also talk to your vet if your pup seems unusually tired, especially if he's still tired after the initial post-op twenty-four hours are up and the anaesthetic has worn off completely.

- Look out for other signs of complications, such as diarrhea, vomiting, problems urinating, pale gums or laboured breathing.

- The cone your pup might be wearing to keep him from chewing and licking his sutures after surgery is like a satellite dish, collecting and amplifying all the noises around him. Don't baby-talk at your pup and be extra respectful of his sensitive canine hearing. Keep all high pitches in check. I suggest that if the collar bugs your pup, give him a break from it periodically by putting him on umbilical, but when the collar's off, you'll have to be watchful of any nipping or licking at the stitches.

Urban Agility Training

Starting at about ten months of age—or sooner with larger-breed pups who like to herd, guard and retrieve (and have also been fixed)—it's time to start urban agility training. This is a great way of making the most of your pup's developing dexterity, coordination and confidence. And agility training is fun. It's a new way of bonding with a pup who needs to express and fulfill her need for independence. But since you'll be starting agility training on umbilical, it also provides an interspecies bond that'll keep your pup dialed in to your leadership capabilities. At the same time, it will show *you* what your pup can do with all her smarts and skills, which both species have worked so hard to foster.

If you were inconsistent in enforcing the household playbook rules or in holding your pup accountable for rebelliousness during the terrible twos—or if you jumped off the training bandwagon—your pup is now going to start throwing around a lot of attitude. What's more, she's become smarter, stronger and faster and might start using her new skill sets to beat you at what she sees as your own leadership "game." And your pup will start playing other games with you, like "Catch me if you can." In dogspeak they're basically saying, "Impress me if you can. I dare you." She will also have mastered the ability to anticipate your next move, so you'll have to step up your speed and agility and get trickier. The goal is to be a few steps ahead of your canine and anticipate any misbehaviours so you can keep the corrections and disciplinary actions to a minimum.

Agility training is ideal because it allows you to dictate movement while still changing things up. And as I've said before, canines love the element of surprise. By introducing agility, you'll catch your pup off guard and that's a great way to curb the adolescent "seen it, done it" world weariness. Show your pup that you can impress her and give her the opportunity to do likewise.

Step-by-Step Urban Agility Training: Weaving, Jumping, Balancing

Urban agility training is similar to teaching an animal how to run an obstacle course except that instead of using a staged course like the ones used in dog competitions, you make use of objects in your neighbourhood: benches, trees, logs, street lamps, stairways, parking curbs, stones, boulders, ramps and playgrounds. You can turn almost any urban or sub-urban environment into an obstacle course. At home you can also set up an impromptu course in your backyard on those days when you have limited time to hang with your pooch. Or do indoor agility

THE SCIENTIFIC SCOOP ON AGILITY TRAINING

Obstacle training, walking on a flat surface and walking uphill are therapeutic for dogs. This was the result of an Austrian study that analyzed the motion of the joints of healthy dogs' fore-limbs and hind limbs during specific exercises.[22] The researchers found that of four exercises conducted, only downhill walking had a less-than-therapeutic impact on dogs' joints. Note that the researchers didn't say that downhill walking is bad for canines, simply that it causes extra stess on a canine's body.

while you do chores, using the stairs and furniture as obstacles. The objective is to find or create a space in which you and your dog can navigate around a lot of objects and change directions frequently.

Check the collar and leash for any cracks or breaks, leash up your pup and get into umbilical. When you leave your house, start off by walking at a slower pace so your pup can pick up some daily news. This will also help warm up your muscles— yours and your canine's. Pick up the pace and start jogging, but get your puppy used to the pace before you really get into it. If there's any strain on the leash, stop and do a leash correction before beginning the agility training. Your pup should be following your lead, not lagging or pulling behind.

Weaving Agility Exercises

1. Start navigating around obstacles together, weaving around things like trees, lamp posts, hydro poles and benches. Assess your

surroundings and weave around anything that works and is safe.

2. Find objects that you can step on and jump down from that suit your pup's height and abilities—like slab benches, logs, large rocks or boulders or playground equipment. Avoid obstacles with slats or gaps larger than your pup's paws.

3. As you approach these obstacles, pick up your speed slightly. Whatever you do, don't hesitate.

4. Step up on the obstacle. Did your pup follow you up? If so, step down to the other side immediately. The goal is to have your feet touch the ground just before your pup's paws touch down. If your pup touches down before you, ramp up your speed as you go on to the next obstacle.

Pup-Friendly Obstacles

Be considerate of your pup's height and ability to navigate tight corners and clear high thresholds. You don't want to force a stubby-legged pup to jump down from heights or make any jarring movements that will cause too much wear and tear on his spine. If your pup can't reach up to an object such as a bench with his front paws, don't use that object as an obstacle for jumping up and over. But if your low rider can jump up on the couch or other off-limits human furniture, he'll be able to get up and down from slab benches.

5. Did your pup stop and refuse to jump up on the obstacle? That might mean that the obstacle is too high. However, the first few times you do agility, your pup might not follow you up and over obstacles even if they're not too high. Don't force the issue if this happens, especially with small pups. Instead, say, "Hustle" in an upbeat tone and open your arms to invite your pup to come up, but never pick him up.

    If your pup didn't jump up this time, step back down and start moving again until there's ample space between you and that obstacle. Pick up the pace as you reapproach the obstacle. Don't hesitate because if you do, your pup will sense that and put on his brakes again.

    Step up on the obstacle again. If your pup puts on the brakes once more, get back down on the ground and, using the leash, guide your pup upward.

6. If your pup continues to resist, focus instead on the weaving agility exercises you did in the first step (above) before attempting any more jumping-up agility exercises.

7. After a few sessions, if your pup continues to resist, get back down on the ground on the other side of the bench and do the Eat the Leash Exercise I introduced you to in Stage 4. As mentioned in Stage 4, eating the leash is like pulling a boat toward a dock by

gradually pulling in more and more of the line (the rope) attached to the boat. You would do that with both of your hands, one hand at a time.

The goal is to guide your pup up and onto the obstacle. If your pup is resistant, the leash will strain as you pull your pup toward you.

8. To keep your pup attentive, continue mixing up your speed as you navigate around and over objects.

9. Whenever there's a strain on the leash, give a quick, concise leash correction, but (as I've mentioned before!), please don't treat the leash like a fishing reel by yanking continually on it, and resist doing what I call "ringing the church bells," which means doing one leash correction after another.

10. Find an obstacle that's like a balance beam (a bleacher or a wide set of stairs, for instance) and, using the leash, guide your pup toward it while you stay at ground level by his side. If she needs to lean on you to balance herself, let her do that and then continue walking beside the obstacle. Keep your pace relatively slow at first, in order to acclimatize your pup to walking the balance beam.

11. Try the balance beam again, increasing your momentum a little bit each time until your

pup increases her dexterity to the point where she can easily walk along the beam.

12. As the dexterity, fluidity of movement and confidence levels of you and your pup improve, add new obstacles to the mix.

13. Change up the settings each time to add excitement and new challenges. Check out different playgrounds (make sure they're pet friendly), urban parks, public squares and even some parking lots (but only when they're empty, of course). As your puppy's agility and focus improves, and if he's been solidly off-leash-trained, start incorporating off-leash agility into the rotation. Don't do all agility exercises all the time, though. Keep on doing the other exercises and games I've described earlier in this book.

Remember that your primary goals as your puppy's caregiver are to bond with your pup in a novel, fun and energetic way; increase your pup's confidence; and allow him to show off his skills. So if you and your pup start to lose focus, mix up the urban agility with play breaks and dog-to-dog socializing. If you get frustrated during the process of introducing your pup to new challenges, end a session doing something you know your pup can do. That way you'll end each session with a win-win. Urban agility will satisfy your pup's growing need for both physical and mental stimulation, and it will also take your bond of mutual trust to new heights and depths.

And bring a "can do" attitude to this training. If you're cool or even lukewarm about agility training, your pup will think you're dull and even incapable, and that's the last thing you want. Do your best not to pass any hesitancy, reserve or even doubtfulness on to your pup about what *he* can do. Have faith in what both species can bring to the relationship!

All in the Family: Puppy Training With Children and Teens

Maybe you have tween-aged or teenaged humans in your interspecies house who are uninterested or zoned out whenever you try to get them to do their chores or even engage with them over the dinner table. Don't let this stop you from getting them involved in the dog-training process! It's so important for every family member to take on a healthy leadership role in a pup's life. And don't forget that two-legged teenagers are also looking for your approval and respect; like pups they want to be useful and accountable. So have your kids accompany you during some of your agility training and off-leash training sessions.

Explain the purpose and techniques behind each exercise and then ask your kids to hold you accountable and true to the rules of assertive body movements; speed; dexterity; and clear, concise, consistent commands. Tell your kids to make you do push-ups every time you make an error—they'll love it! You can even have them record your agility sessions on their cameras or smartphones so you can

watch the footage together and note your own hiccups and mistakes.

Teens think they know best, but if you explain to
them the importance of initial imprinting and training and that the quality of their puppy's life depends
on following the rules, they usually get right on
board. Assign daily, scheduled canine duties to them,
like covering the morning or late-afternoon walk,
feeding the pup and scooping backyard poop, but
also put them in charge of some of the play sessions—
like the hide-and-seek or tug and retrieval games.

Another great idea is to get your kids to do your
daily duties so you can walk the dog or chill out solo
or as a couple. Get the kids to cook dinner or do
housework while they have the pup on umbilical.
Trust in your kids' abilities to do things right, and
they'll find that hanging with the dog can be a
reward too.

If you have kids in your life who are younger than
twelve years old, I hope you took my earlier advice
(in Stage 4, for instance) and included them during
the initial training and bonding phases. I hope
they've also learned to follow your household playbook. As they mature, they can take on more and
more responsibilities and engage with your pup,
doing activities they prefer. Kids are especially great
doing agility training with low-rider pups because
they themselves might also have trouble getting up
and over obstacles. (Have them focus on weaving
around objects with the pup instead.) Again, use
your discretion, but include your kids in your pup's
agility and umbilical training.

STAGE 10

you've come a long way, puppy: celebrating your pup's first year

Your pup's first birthday is just around the corner, and the honeymoon period, when your cute, innocent little puppy shadowed you and fixated adoringly on your every move, now seems like a distant memory. It could be tempting, during this final two-month period of your pup's first year, to ignore your pup's unique, new view of the world. But don't give in to that! If you do, you'll not only miss out on another important stage, you could actually strain the bond you and your pup have worked so hard to establish. Many people are lured into glorifying the early phase and engage in selective amnesia about all the past challenges. Some

BRAD PATTISON'S PUPPY BOOK

might even be considering bringing a new puppy into the mix—but I would discourage that.

To help you tune in to your almost-one-year-old pup, here are a few more advanced games. And when the year is up, throw your pup a surprise first birthday by trying a new off-leash activity that suits his unique personality as you've come to know, love and admire it over the past year.

Biking With Your Puppy

Biking is a great way to explore new places with your canine, but before you start riding, your pup needs to be solidly off-leash-trained, and she needs to understand one hundred percent that you're the boss and that she must heed the movements of *all* humans. Think about it: if your pup gets in the way of another cyclist, it could be a disaster, so ask yourself these questions before you even think about introducing this new activity:

- Can your pup sit-stay for at least five minutes?

- When your pup is off-leash, does she stop on a dime after a "Stop" directive?

- Does your pup rarely (or never) cause leash friction during umbilical training, agility training or any walks on-leash?

- Does your pup respect the leadership of all humans in dictating movements?

- Does your pup yield to your feet during the Toe Tap Game?

If the answer is a resounding yes to *all of the above questions*, then it's time to start teaching your puppy how to steer clear of bike tires. If not, continue with all the training and bonding I've discussed in previous chapters until you're completely sure that your pup is ready for this. Remember that it's always safety first when introducing your pup to new challenges.

Biking Preparedness: The Tire Test

Start out with a modified version of the Toe Tap Game:

1. Stand square to your pup and move one foot toward her front paws.

2. Did your pup shuffle backward immediately? Excellent! Give her a chest scrunch.

3. If your pup continues to stand there like a stump, let your foot make contact with her paw and press down ever so slightly, to put gentle pressure on one paw. At this point your pup should pull her paws away.

4. If your pup doesn't yield this time, she isn't ready for biking. Focus on off-leash, umbilical and agility training for at least a few weeks before you try again.

5. If your pup did back off when you applied slight pressure, continue with the Toe Tap Game daily until your pup's paws retreat *every time* as soon as you make a move to tap her paws.

Next, bring your bike out to the driveway, the backyard or some other outdoor spot.

1. Stand beside your bike and push it toward your pup at strolling speed.

2. The goal is for your pup to treat the bike tire like your feet and get out of the way.

3. If she doesn't get out of the way, grab onto the bike handles and hold the bike up so the front wheel is floating just above the ground as you continue moving toward your pup.

4. If she continues to stay put, the bike wheel will make contact with her. Remember that it's her responsibility to get out of the way; it's not your responsibility to move her. But you might have to exert slight pressure against your pup's body before she understands the message.

Now try the exercise again from the top. Your pup should be steering clear of that bike tire consistently. If you find your pup wants to eat the tire, keep doing the exercise until that tire doesn't seem like prey to her.

The *Tour de Puppy*: Biking

For your first few biking sessions, do only short dis-
tances and gradually work up to longer rides. Think
of it as a fun opportunity to do another activity with
your pup, but be respectful of her physical abilities.
Choose a quiet neighbourhood or even a large, flat
soccer field. Leash your pup up, but let the leash drag.

Start with the bike tire test,
and if your pup passes, give her a
chest scrunch and say, "Let's
go." As you're biking, your pup
shouldn't run too close beside
you. Allow your pup to enjoy her
freedom, but stop if she gets too
far ahead of you or lags too far
behind. This seems simple and
straightforward because it is!
They key is the bond you've already nurtured with your puppy
and the level of trust and understanding you've developed.

> ### *Bike Leash-Free*
>
> Never attach a leashed
> pup to your handlebars
> and never hold the
> leash with one hand.
> Set-ups like this are
> accidents waiting to
> happen.

The second time you go for a ride, de-collar your
pup, but put the collar and leash in your pocket in
case you need them. Stick to quiet neighbourhoods
close to home until you're comfortable with the activity and then graduate to longer rides. You can
even try mountain biking if you like. For longer and
more strenuous rides, take water and a collapsible
water dish and choose areas with lots of shade and
water sources for your pup to cool off. Take a break
periodically to stretch yourself and let your pup rest
and also to monitor her breathing. If her breathing is

laboured or if she's panting profusely or drooling more than usual or if she seems tired, take a longer break before heading back, and make sure you don't bike too fast.

Puppy Vocabulary:
Show, Tell and Fetch!

Have you heard about the Border collie named Rico who could understand more than two hundred words? That's impressive bilingualism! Rico was tutored by behavioural scientists who claimed that he was able to retrieve the correct item thirty-seven out of forty times—an impressive stat.[23] His owners started instructing him at ten months, so why not start with your pup now? But please remember, this is a game! Don't treat your pup like your own private lab rat.

1. Get down on the ground with your pup and his three toys.

2. Spread the toys out in front of him. Point to one of the toys and give it a simple name like "Bob." Repeat the name a few times.

3. Do the same for the other two toys, always pointing at each specific toy while you say its name.

4. After you've repeated the name of each toy several times, stand up and step back and

ask your pup to "Fetch Bob" in an upbeat
tone.

5. Try not to look at the toy you're referring to.
Stay focused on your pup so you don't accidentally cue your pup to that toy.

6. Once your pup consistently has a handle on
the names of the toys, put him in a sit-stay,
choose the "Bob" toy and then leave the room
and place the toy in an easy-to-find spot.

7. When you come back, say, "Fetch Bob" and
point to the room where you hid the toy.

8. When your pup returns with the toy, praise
your pooch with a chest scrunch and have a
play session with that toy.

9. If your dog comes back confused, put him
back in a sit-stay and repeat the exercise. Go
into the other room, but this time place the
toy in plain sight.

10. If your dog remains attentive, repeat the
game with another toy.

11. As your pup gets the hang of this type of
hide-and-seek, start using two toys at a time
and asking your pup to fetch one of the toys.
Be sure to hold up each of the toys and
name them one at a time before you hide
one of them.

TAKE YOUR TIME
AND ENJOY!

Don't be too surprised if it takes some time for your pup to attach meaning to the names of the toys and respond to your request to fetch. Some pups are instinctual learners and others are repetitive learners. The repetitive learners will need to play the game many times before they learn the names and understand the requests. And when dogs are tired or stoked to play or romp around, they'll be much less attentive. Ditto for you, so if you're tired, impatient, frustrated or inattentive, skip the game and go for a walk.

12. Put the other toy in your pocket or in another out-of-reach place for the first few sessions. Then, as your pup's skills improve, hide both toys and see if he can differentiate between the two.

Games like this should be fun activities that stimulate your pup's mind. Canines only really need to know about twenty words and phrases or so to get along in the domestic pack. And that includes the basic training directives ("Sit," "Stay," "Hustle" and "Stop") and behavioural cues (including a word or phrase they identify with sleeping, chilling out or resisting negative behaviours like trashing your possessions and repetitive barking). Dogs communicate primarily through their scent and body language, so that's why I keep reminding you that you need to be bilingual in dogspeak. That is, besides using verbal commands, you need to use body language.

The Shell Game

This game will engage your pup's mind, and it's a bit like Show-and-Tell.

1. Grab one of your pup's toys and three pillows or three opaque bowls that can cover the toy (serving as "shells").

2. Now put your pup in a sit-stay.

3. Place each of the three "shells" about three feet (one metre) in front of her, with about a two-foot (half-metre) distance between each shell.

4. Sit square to your pup behind the middle shell. Then pick up the toy, show it to your pup and tell her its verbal word tag (such as "Ball" if that is what the toy is).

5. Next, hold up that toy and place it under one of the shells.

6. Then say, "Fetch the ball" in an upbeat tone. (Don't gaze or look at the shell covering the ball. Keep your eyes on your pup.)

7. Did your pup uncover the correct shell to get that ball? If so, reward her with a chest scrunch.

8. Repeat the exercise, placing the ball under another shell.

9.   Do this a few times until your pup is consistently locating the ball on the first try.

10.   Now do the same exercise, but this time, put the ball in the shell *on the left*.

11.   Point and look at the shell *on the right* and say, "Fetch the ball" as you continue to point at the incorrect shell.

12.   Did your pup look at the correct shell but choose the shell you were pointing and gazing at? That's actually the norm for dogs, based on scientific experiments. Even though your dog understands that the ball is under a specific shell, your cues as the dog's owner and caregiver—your leadership cues of pointing, gazing and suggesting—dictated the choice of the wrong shell. Researchers have found that when left to make the decision by themselves, dogs will pick the correct shell but when directed otherwise by their owners, they'll follow our lead. They'll depend on *our* guidance and behave according to our directions, even if those directions are counterproductive. They do this because they're smart enough to adapt their choices to suit us.

I hope that's an "aha!" for you, and I hope that it helps you understand that if you're providing any negative or counterproductive guidance, education and leadership, your pup will follow your lead—for better or worse. So choose the better and give good guidance!

Choice Pups:
Requesting Actions and Behaviours

So far, the training and bonding methods in this book have been geared toward educating your pup so he can get along in our domestic sphere and follow our well-balanced lead. By now, you should have a thorough grasp of the power of confident, assertive body language; quick, concise movements; and clean, simple verbal and nonverbal directives and commands. Now that your pup is about to turn one and has gradually earned the way to greater freedoms and liberties, it's time to add another reward to the mix. It's time to start using verbal *requests* (as opposed to commands). This is about putting a question mark at the end of a directive instead of commanding your pup—it's about providing your pup with a choice.

This might seem contradictory to my training style, and I'm certainly not saying that from now on you will never have to use assertive, firm commands with your pup. However, the twelve-month age may actually be an important benchmark for your relationship, marking a shift from commanding to *requesting* specific skills and behaviours. That said, even if your dog is about twelve months old, he might not be ready for you to start making requests as well as commands. In fact, even when your pet is fully mature, you'll always need to mix up basic training with advanced training and safeguard him against potential harms. Expectations, challenges, learning opportunities and surprises are so important for dogs, just as they are for people. But security and going back to review old rules or to do simpler things are also needed for your pet's well-being.

If your one-year-old pup has yet to get a grasp of basic training and still pulls on the leash unnecessarily or if you've yet to make progress with off-leash training, I suggest holding off on teaching him requests. Focus instead on Hustle training, which also incorporates the element of choice in a positive and fun-loving way. Then, once your pup can do that consistently and has also learned to stop on a dime, you're ready to start adding requests to the mix.

Start tacking a question mark onto your verbal directives about simple activities like "Ready to eat?" or "Walk?" Your pup might respond with a quick bark or show some sign of enthusiasm, but I highly doubt that he'll shrug, yawn and stroll away. Next, start mixing in training-related requests like "Sit?" when you're out on a walk and you stop to chat with a neighbour or answer your cellphone.

Take it slow. Once your pup masters biking, you can ask, "Do you want to go biking? or to the dog park?" Add a gesture as well. Say, "Biking?" as you bounce one hand up and down and then "Dog park" as you bounce the other hand up and down. Maybe your pup will already be able to indicate his preference with a bark or a gaze at one of your hands.

Choices can overwhelm any canine, so if your one-year-old is not ready for these activities, wait until he is. In general, pups reach social maturity at two years old and emotional maturity at the age of about three. By that point, but no sooner, you can start introducing additional choices from time to time by inviting your pup to do things that you shouldn't even think about asking during the early developmental phase. For instance, you might *occasionally* invite a mature dog with an excellent track record of good behaviour and a compliant attitude to join you on the couch (but never, ever your bed, please!). Remember that you should always be in control of any situation like this. Invitations and requests should always be dictated by your leadership. Whatever your dog's age, he should always accommodate and act upon your requests and directions.

Remember to be patient and upbeat about your individual pup's current skills. Like people, dogs have different areas of strength, but they can all benefit from stretching their skill levels and learning to be contented members of the human pack. I hope you'll have a long life together because the road is long and wide and full of great times. Whenever you run into hurdles, get back on umbilical and do refresher courses covering all the training techniques in this book. But don't get stuck in any routine ruts. Use the element of surprise to harness your pup's curiosity and satisfy that dogged detective!

EPILOGUE
positive interspecies empowerment

For me, dog training is about so much more than sterile obedience training. It's about sharing my life with dogs. It's as much about learning about myself as understanding my canine companions. And that's another reason why I'm constantly taking risks and putting myself out there to learn more. I also look at each puppy as an individual. Many people in my young industry are more interested in the financial bottom line. I don't understand that because each puppy represents a life with so much potential, and each life should have the support of a domestic pack and an entire community. Unfortunately, this is not the focus of many people in my industry, who are dominated by negativity, corruption, selfishness, ego and nastiness. They don't see puppies and dogs as individuals who can contribute to the emotional and social well-being of those around them. Instead, these lovable, smart, curious animals are treated like robots that can be turned on and off with a treat or a clicker or some other ridiculous and dangerous gimmick.

I am creating a community of tenacious, dedicated dog industry stakeholders—my league of Certified Trainer Educators, stellar vets, the pet stores that carry my line of Hustle Up™ products—and most of all, the people and dogs that I've worked with and met during one-on-one training, seminars and 6Legs to Fitness sessions. The fact that so many people have trusted me with their canines speaks volumes, and it keeps me humble and motivated to do better. The goal is to enlarge that community and provide positive support for people and pups. I'm always striving to learn more because it's tomorrow that matters. It's all the tomorrows of your pup's young life. Why can't we all do our best for them? In the process, that dedication will pay off in our lives and our communities, in huge emotional gains.

I hope that you'll add your voice and energy to our mission. It might be by helping a neighbour-hood family with a dog whose canine needs are neglected, by inviting them to do some training sessions with you or volunteering to dog-sit. Maybe you'll check my blog and start interacting with me there. Or participate in one of my seminars or training courses. Maybe you'll look into legislation around puppy mills or decide to enroll in my dog-training school. Whatever you do, I hope this book provided you with some inspiration. But most important, I hope that your puppy inspires you.

Every day is the beginning of a new set of adventures for puppies. Celebrate your successes, acknowledge your errors and challenges, and grow from them. Believe you can do anything you put your mind to. Remove words like "can't" or "won't" or "I'll try"—and say, "I will" instead! Your pup is always rooting for you. That's one of the things I love most about dogs. I rarely meet a canine that doesn't embrace action. Of course, in the wrong hands, that dogged curiosity and trustfulness can get them into a lot of trouble. Don't let that happen to yourself and your pup. Be positively empowered so that you can continue to empower your pup.

To me, one of the great pleasures in life happens when a pup seeks me out and plops one of his favourite toys in front of me as an invitation to engage, let loose, have some fun. Or invites me for a game of chase. Those ears spring up and that tail starts clocking back and forth—that body language is like a big, goofy smile. Pups are always creating these golden opportunities with people. Don't ignore the invitations. Listen to what these small actions and gestures mean, and act on them.

I'm truly honoured that you were open to learning about my ideas and methods. All of the techniques and philosophies are meant to be used and adapted throughout your pup's entire life, and I trust that you will continue to strive for success by taking your training and bonding to new heights. Once your pup is off-leash trained and is mature enough to be safe and trustworthy, you'll be able to let your pup take the lead while *you* follow. Isn't that the ultimate empowerment? Be open, engaged and curious about what your pup can teach and show you.

Now it's *your* turn to take the skills and techniques you've learned in this book and incorporate them into your family pack. Take it to the next level. I'll always be rooting for you. Now, let's get out there — let's get off-leash!

APPENDIX
puppy development chart and chapter recaps

PUPPY DEVELOPMENT CHART

AGE	CANINE BEHAVIOURS	CANINE NEEDS	TRAINING/BONDING ACTIVITIES
Stage 1 Birth to 8 Weeks	• Initially blind & deaf; can't regulate body temperature, bowels, hygiene • Feeding, weaning • Taught to eliminate outside canine pen • Playing with siblings, learning canine etiquette	• To be with the canine mom/litter until the age of 8 weeks • To learn the rules, boundaries & structure of the canine pack • Gradual initial exposure to humans	• Pre-pet counselling • Never buy your pet from a puppy mill or backyard breeder or from most pet shops • Investigate your prospective pup's breeder or shelter • Research breed traits for compatibility with you • Avoid trendy training methods (e.g., treats, clickers, shock collars)

AGE	CANINE BEHAVIOURS	CANINE NEEDS	TRAINING/BONDING ACTIVITIES
Stage 2 8 weeks	• Curious, playful, energetic • Looking to you for all caregiving, leadership • Sleeps most of the time • If removed from the litter prior to 8 weeks, will already have negative behaviours like barking, trashing, separation anxiety	• High-protein puppy food, fresh water (no treats, human food or foods poisonous to canines) • Calm, low-pitched human voices; more body language than talk • Introduction to rules & boundaries of your human pack • Acclimatization to the pup's new personal space (crate/bed/3 toys) • Acclimatization to peeing & pooping zone • Socialization/play to build physical & emotional skills • To be respected & treated as a dog, not humanized or infantilized	• Puppy-proof your home • Buy leash, collar, dog bed & crate, grooming & bathing supplies • Buy 3 toys for pup • Remember pup is being introduced to foreign pack (human pack) • Learn to speak canine: vigilance about negative human body language & your tone of voice • Identify peeing & pooping spot • Feed good raw food or high-protein puppy food • Buy food & water bowls • Introduce dog to crate • Teach kids to respect pup

Stage		Behavior	Needs	Activities
Stage 3 8–11 weeks (2–2.5 months)		• Plays "nonstop" & bounces around you • Attentive to your verbal communication, body language, gestures, movements • Teething, chewing, mouthing, sucking • Engages you to play, wrestle, grapple	• Maintenance of consistent rules & boundaries of your human pack • To understand & respect that all humans are the boss (no human mixed messages) • To acclimatize to elimination zone • To be left alone when eating • Lots of play & mental stimulation • Continued habituation to human touch (e.g., massage) • Socialization with other dogs & people	• Introduce pup to his 3 toys • Be consistent in house-training, (bladder control in increasing increments) • Paw-Grappling Game • Do first chest scrunch • Do full body massage • Teach to sleep in own bed (first bedtime)

AGE	CANINE BEHAVIOURS	CANINE NEEDS	TRAINING/BONDING ACTIVITIES
Stage 4 8–11 weeks (2–2.5 months [cont'd])	• Pup sleeps a lot • When awake, plays nonstop • At about 11 weeks, will follow you around • May resist being collared and leashed • Is so curious, she may destroy things accidentally as she investigates • Will chew, teeth, nip and mouth • Wants to socialize • Could either be aggressive with children or get along well • Will resist leash if has behavioural issues	• Rules & boundaries • To develop trust in your leadership & dependability as a caregiver • Nonverbal communication • To be habituated to the leash/your leadership & control (especially if she is a leash hater) • Daily walks & mental stimulation • To socialize with other dogs/people • Accountability for negative behaviours • No long, emotional goodbyes & hellos • To gradually acclimatize to being alone	• Initial umbilical training • Umbilical training with kids • Eat the Leash Exercise for leash haters • Consistent chew training with Tug O' War Game • Learn to groom pup • Give puppy first bath • Initial patience training to increase your pup's comfort while home alone

Stage 5 11–15 weeks (2.5–3.5 months)	• At 15 weeks, will start taking the lead when walking with you • Tends to follow directions easily • Type of learner begins to emerge (instinctual/repetitive)	• To satisfy curiosity (is "doggy detective") • A lot of mental stimulation • To socialize with other dogs • Increased outdoor exercise, play & mental stimulation to satisfy curiosity, prevent boredom	• Do Sit, Stay, Hustle & Stop training • Street safety training • Vehicle safety training • Praise each success (make it a win-win for you & pup) • Always cap training sessions with positive play • Teach dog park etiquette & take to dog park • Learn about & prevent heat stroke • After vaccination, take pup to pet store to shop for 3 new toys

241

AGE	CANINE BEHAVIOURS	CANINE NEEDS	TRAINING/BONDING ACTIVITIES
Stage 6 15–22 weeks (3.5–5 months)	• Starts taking the lead • Pulls at the leash • Personality begins to emerge • Breed behaviour may emerge (e.g., nipping, herding, fetching, hunting) • Fixations, phobias may emerge	• Understand that you're the boss in dogspeak (you communicate through assertive, concise body movements & leadership capabilities) • More outdoor exercise • More mental stimulation	• Alpha Test (embrace your alpha position) • Advanced umbilical training to bond with & train pup & ramp up your dogspeak skills • Learn & do leash correction techniques geared to the strength/size of your pup • Toe Tap Game • Puppy Yoga • Education about puppy fixations & phobias
Stage 7 5–7 months	• Starts to lose "puppy" look • Always takes the lead • Ramps up the alpha attitude	• Craves the freedom of off-leash canine interactions • Needs a leader who's fun & engaging	• Do off-leash training starting in an enclosed space & gradually more challenging places like the dog park & the street

	• Personality starts to blossom • May show signs of separation anxiety	• Needs praise for doing something right; accountability for doing something wrong	• Midterm test of your puppy magnetism • Advanced patience training (to curb separation anxieties) • Hide-and-Seek Game
Stage 8 7–9 months (the Terrible Twos)	• Continually pushes the boundaries • Tantrums, meltdowns, manipulative tactics, misbehaviours • Rebels against training, commands to sit-stay, etc. • Always looking to score a win • Personality blossoms	• Refresher courses on all basic training • To be put back on leash • Your concentrated leadership & also your understanding of instinctual canine behaviours • Your respect of all canine needs, skills • To learn to be accountable for misbehaviours, antics	• Re-leash your pup • Do umbilical for 2 weeks • No-Talking Playbook (no talking to your pup for 2 weeks) • Interruption & correction techniques • No new training • Education about why canines jump up, bark excessively & trash possessions • The Peck Fake-Out • The Hand Throw Down • The Timeout

AGE	CANINE BEHAVIOURS	CANINE NEEDS	TRAINING/BONDING ACTIVITIES
Stage 9 9–10 months	• Puppy cutes gone • Not physically or emotionally mature • Dexterity, coordination & confidence are developing	• To be spayed or neutered • Your attention, respect & mutual trust • New mental & physical stimulation • Craves new experiences, freedom, new places	• Get pup spayed or neutered (no rigorous exercise for about 2 weeks) • Urban Agility Training • Training with kids/teens
Stage 10 10–12 months	• Individual personality is fully formed (likes, dislikes, traits, skills) • Breed-related traits well established • Responds well to firm commands	• Craves independence, new friends, new environments, novelty in general • Praise & respect for skills & talents • Will respect your leadership, for better and for worse	• Do Bike Safety Training (including the Tire Test) • Show-and-Tell (expanded verbal vocabulary) • The Shell Game (testing your pup's trust in you) • Introduce the concept of requests, choice • Celebrate 1st birthday with a "surprise": a brand-new outdoor activity

STAGE 1 RECAP: WHAT A PUPPY NEEDS

- Conduct a do-it-yourself pre–pet counselling session to identify whether you're puppy material. Be honest about your strengths and limitations, your available resources, your daily rituals, your personality, skill sets and interests.
- Think long and hard about basic canine needs and whether you're willing and able to meet those needs every day of your pup's entire life, including becoming the pack leader.
- Do your necessary homework investigating breeders, pet store pups, shelter pups and breed compatibility so you can find the ideal pup for you.
- Do not buy a pup from any puppy mill or a backyard breeder.
- If you decide to go with a breeder, please read my Breeder Questionnaire and Breeder Meet-and-Greet information in the Resources section at the end of this book.
- Never purchase a puppy that has been removed from the litter before the age of eight weeks.
- Be extremely wary of trendy dog-training methods, such as so-called "positive reinforcement" treat and clicker training. These methods are one-trick ponies that dismiss and disempower canine and human smarts.

STAGE 2 RECAP: PUPPY PREPAREDNESS

Refer to this puppy preparedness checklist often:
- Puppy-proof your home to create a safe environment for your pup that also minimizes the potential

risk of your pup trashing your human possessions.

- Invest in a good raw puppy food or high-protein dry puppy food.

- Invest in basic puppy supplies: a leash and Martingale collar; a dog bed and crate; three puppy toys; and grooming and bathing supplies.

- Keep your pup's canine needs in mind as you prime yourself for your pup's arrival. Embrace the impending excitement, but maintain a healthy, well-balanced attitude and do your best to tap into and mesh with the canine point of view.

- Learn truly positive strategies for training and bonding by learning to speak canine. This way you can dial into your pup's innate canine smarts and skills and better understand the world from your pup's unique viewpoint.

STAGE 3 RECAP: WELCOME TO THE (HUMAN) JUNGLE: PUPPY'S FIRST TWENTY-FOUR HOURS IN YOUR PACK

Here's a roundup of training methods and caregiving activities to start you off on the right foot.

- Ideally, when you first bring your new pup home, book off a long weekend or cash in a week or two of vacation time so you can spend as much time as possible bonding with your puppy.

- When it comes to bonding with your new puppy, keep the chatter to a minimum; don't overwhelm your pup with a lot of verbal requests and orders; and don't use any high-pitched baby talk.

- Resist picking up your puppy excessively. Let her take in the smells, sounds and sights of her new 'hood from the canine point of view—the *ground*—right from the start and every day after that.

- Feed your pup only puppy food—no human food. Leave her alone when she eats, and make the kitchen area a no-play zone.
- Make sure your pup has his own chill zone, bed and crate so he has his own spots for relaxing and sleeping. Introduce your pup to that zone and let him learn how to relax and go to sleep.
- Don't let your pup become accustomed to sitting on any human furniture, including your bed.
- Start house-training immediately. Keep an elimination diary, so you can discover how long your pup can hold her bladder.
- Allow a few accidents with a young pup, especially as he learns how to eliminate outdoors and gains control of his bladder. But make sure to teach your pup or adult dog that such behaviour is unacceptable.
- Learn how to give your pup a chest scrunch, a full-body massage and a mouth massage so you can get to know her body and so she becomes habituated to human touch. This is also the ideal way to reward your pup in the most positive way possible—through kind and caring actions.
- Play with your pup so he sees you as a fun caregiver.

STAGE 4 RECAP: PUPPY IMPRINTING: UMBILICAL TRAINING, CHEW TRAINING AND GROOMING

Here's a round-up of things you need to do during your puppy's first three weeks in your pack, whether she's eight to eleven weeks of age or weeks or months older.

- Maintain consistent house-training.
- Start umbilical training with your pup and practise it every day for at least two weeks.
- If your tenacious pup refuses to be walked on-leash, do the Eat the Leash Exercise described in Stage 4 until your pup gets used to your control on-leash.
- Begin the Tug o' War Game (described in Stage 4) to introduce chew training so your pup learns to habituate to the human hand. This exercise will also engage your pup's need for mental stimulation and play, and it will teach your pup that he has free rein over his three toys but not your human possessions.
- If your pup trashes your human possessions, she must be sent a clear message that such home wrecking is not acceptable and that she is accountable for her negative actions.
- Introduce your pup to her first bath.
- Groom your pet to ward off matting and other potential health issues and to strengthen your bond.
- Massage your pup regularly.
- Start introducing your pup to people and to other well-behaved, vaccinated, healthy dogs of a variety of ages.

- Whenever you leave your pup alone, refrain from engaging in long, emotionally charged goodbyes and hellos. This means minimal to no talking and minimal touching.
- Acclimatize your pup to being comfortable on her own by leaving home a short time at first and then gradually increasing the amount of time you're away.
- Have your pup vaccinated when she's about two and a half months old. Once she's vaccinated, you can start cruising the dog parks and meeting new two- and four-legged friends.

STAGE 5 RECAP: THE HONEYMOON PERIOD: STREET SAFETY TRAINING

Remember that we're all works in progress: nobody's perfect, and perfection is boring anyway. But your pup does need to learn a number of things for his own safety and for your and his well-being. Here are some basic training sessions and strategies:

- Begin teaching your pup to sit, stay, hustle and stop. Always end each session with praise and a good play romp.
- Start street-proofing your pup with street safety training.
- Give your pup the time and patience to learn at his own speed. Remember that many, many pups are repetitive learners and need a lot of time and consistency with training. Have faith that he will master a skill when he's ready, and meanwhile, mix up training with loads of fun activities, old and new.

- Teach your pup how to get in and out of your vehicle.
- Always be mindful of the potential hazards of parking lots.
- Take your pup to the dog park so she can meet new canine friends and speak her own canine language daily.
- Educate yourself about the signs of heat stroke during the dog days of summer.
- Take your pup to the pet store to pick three new toys (for chewing, for playing tug and for fetch and retrieval). These should replace the ones you picked out for her before she came home.
- Expose your pup to as many people, places and things as possible to prevent phobias and anxieties (which limit your pup's amazing potential and dogged curiosity).

STAGE 6 RECAP: WHO'S THE BOSS? ASSERTIVE LEADERSHIP SKILLS

Polish up your alpha leadership skills to highlight the fact that you're in control as a trustworthy, caring, considerate pack leader.

- Embrace your position in the spotlight as the alpha of the interspecies pack.
- Conduct an alpha assessment to see if your young pup or mature dog has already started exhibiting alpha tendencies.
- Ramp up the umbilical exercises so your pup learns to follow your lead all the time. Remember that using assertive, consistent movement is the ideal way to "talk" to your pup, so that the message

is understood and respected. As your pup becomes more and more dialed in to your physical movements, you'll be learning to speak each other's first languages.

- Master the leash correction technique. Remember that the goal is to use fast, brief movements in order to make each correction count. That way you won't have to make corrections often. Remember that less is more. It could take some time for you to master this technique, so if you must, practise on other people, but never practise on a canine.
- Remember that you're not correcting your pup just to dominate and power-trip.
- Play the Toe Tap Game to continue acclimatizing your pup to your leadership skills and to build up trust in a fun, positive and upbeat way.
- Learn puppy yoga so your pup's growing limbs, joints and muscles stay healthy.
- Be mindful of your pup's heightened sensitivity to full moons, storms and any loud noises and foreign objects that move in a way that's unnatural from his point of view.
- Remember to have fun and cherish the hiccups, mistakes and quirks as your pup's breed traits and unique personality start to shine.

STAGE 7 RECAP: OFF-LEASH PUPPY POWER

By the time your pup turns seven months old, he should be off-leashed-trained, or close to it. Don't stress over the setbacks. Look at each training session as a success because each one builds on your foundation and also satisfies your pup or mature dog's canine needs—and that means progress from the canine point of view. If you remain patient, upbeat and consistent, you'll start to see all training sessions (including the ones that are less than perfect) as progress.

- Introduce your canine to off-leash training, starting with the basics and ramping up to including off-leash Hustle training, off-leash dog park training and eventually off-leash street safety training.

- Celebrate each success and reward your pup with physical praise, games, wrestling and lots of outdoor exercise.

- Take note of your pup's budding personality as you give her the freedom to express herself in dogspeak (with other dogs and without your intervention) and with the human pack.

- If you hit some road bumps, be willing to get honest with yourself about whether you're neglecting your pup's needs, providing inconsistent training (which overwhelms pups with too many mixed messages) or exposing your canine to too much human stress (such as impatience, fear and negativity), which limits both species' capabilities. Be aware that these negative emotions project onto dogs, and while they might seem subtle to the humans, canines are highly tuned animals and they're dogged detectives when it comes to sniffing out bad vibes.

- Test your puppy magnetism by staying at a distance and then hiding behind a tree or the like while your pup is playing with other dogs in the park. If your pup looks for you, you'll know she thinks you're a fun-loving and energetic caregiver and buddy. By being an engaging, playful buddy, you'll be able to dial in to and harness your pup's unique smarts, skills and energy in the most positive way.

- Patience-train your pup or mature dog, especially if your canine exhibits separation-related anxiety. Be willing and ready to identify and refrain from any negative human traits and behaviours that foster learned helplessness or canine insecurities.
- Play hide-and-seek at home while one-on-one (to continue acclimatizing your pup to sit-stay and being comfortable while you're out of sight). Do this with your pup and with other people— especially kids. Mix up the hide-and-seek game with outdoor training and exercise to maintain your bond.

STAGE 8 RECAP: THE TERRIBLE TWOS: DIVAS, REBELS AND CANINE ACCOUNTABILITY

As you and your pup go through the terrible twos, remind yourself that this stage will pass shortly (in about four weeks) as long as you pull up your bootstraps and embrace your leadership. Here's a snapshot of what healthy leadership looks like during this phase.

- Expect quite a few hiccups and speed bumps during this phase of your pup's life.
- Don't initiate any new training, and put off-leash training on hold for four weeks, so as not to overstimulate and confuse your pup.
- Keep your pup on-leash during all outdoor activities unless you're in secure, fenced-in locations.

- Do two weeks of umbilical combined with two weeks of no talking, in order to harness and dial in to your pup's viewpoint via dogspeak (body language, movement, actions and gestures) and minimize the potential for frustration and rude, stress-related *human* barking and hollering.
- Apply the no-talking rule to all the humans in the household. Communicate nonverbally as much as possible.
- Understand and empathize with why pups and dogs need to explore their boundaries and also why they engage in negative behaviours like jumping up, barking, chewing and digging. Canines do these things instinctually and many have been bred and encouraged to herd, hunt, guard and retrieve.
- In the domestic pack, many instinctual canine behaviours are unacceptable. Puppies need to learn to be accountable for their actions, so it's important to use my methods for interrupting and correcting any unruly behaviours *all the time*— consistently and firmly.
- Be watchful and proactive about any puppy attempts to dethrone you from your necessary position as leader of the pack. Look out for overt manipulation tactics like nipping and territorial aggressiveness, as well as passive-aggressive antics like whining, pouting, begging or engaging in fake submissiveness.
- Be sure to provide your pup with lots of exercise, mental stimulation and socialization.
- Bring a huge reserve of patience into the mix, but don't be a big sack of concrete. Yes, you're building

a foundation, but you'll need a good sense of humour to make the most of teaching, bonding and learning about your pup's personality.

STAGE 9 RECAP: THE JUVENILE PERIOD: URBAN AGILITY TRAINING AND BONDING

The primary goal for this period of your pup's life (aged about nine to ten months) is to keep your pup engaged with you as he navigates through another challenging period of early life. Stay tuned in to your pup and tap into his canine view of the world by getting out there and moving with your pup. Remember that momentum is crucial to all canines and it's especially important during this "teen" period.

- Don't succumb to "empty nest syndrome" (nostalgia for the early puppy days) simply because your pup is maturing and is well on the road to adulthood. Your pup is right there in front of you, yearning to engage and explore the world.
- Have your pup spayed or neutered.
- Start doing urban agility training to dial up your pup's focus, complement his increasing dexterity, physical coordination and confidence.
- Urban agility will give your pup the opportunity to show off her canine skills and *teach you* a few things about life from the canine viewpoint. It will also bring your bond to a new level of mutual trust and respect and help you master your dog-speak bilingualism skills.
- Get your kids to take on responsibility for umbilical training while doing household chores, for

instance, so they can enjoy hanging with the family's pup.

STAGE 10 RECAP:
YOU'VE COME A LONG WAY, PUPPY:
CELEBRATING YOUR PUP'S FIRST YEAR

You'll have many more milestones in the future, but now is the time to celebrate your bond. Celebrate the successes and challenges you've shared this past year and be proud that you and your pup have put in so much effort. It'll pay off in spades as you move forward.

- Train your pup to go off-leash with you while you're biking, starting with acclimatizing your pup to consistently yielding to bike tires in order to prevent and minimize the potential dangers of bike-related accidents.

- Grow your pup's understanding of words and phrases by engaging in the Show-and-Tell Game, using your pup's toys.

- Do the Shell Game to test your pup's smarts and also those dog–human cooperation skills. Remember that a well-trained dog will follow your lead even if she's the smart one and you're wrong.

- Start adding requests and invitations to your verbal and nonverbal communication with your pup. Remember that the element of choice is empowering, rewarding and necessary for both species. As you continue to educate, learn from and bond with each other, pace yourself and your pup so you can enjoy the precious days, months and years ahead.

- Have a big party mixer with your pup and invite some two- and four-legged friends to celebrate your first year together. You've both come a long way!

resources

The Breeder Questionnaire

If you decide to go with a breeder, please do your homework in advance to ensure that the breeder is reputable. Start by interviewing breeders by phone, covering the following questions and concerns. This questionnaire also includes pointers that will help you identify whether a breeder is legit.

1. Is the breeder strict about not allowing you to purchase a pup younger than eight weeks of age? If the breeder allows you to pick up the pup any earlier, cross that one off your list.
2. Does the breeder team up with pet stores. If so, they're a no-go.
3. How long have they been breeding dogs, and do they raise a variety of breeds? Ideally, a breeder will specialize in one specific

breed and will have years or decades of experience with it.

4. What is the age of your prospective pup's canine mom and how many previous litters has she had? She should be at least two years old and no older than seven. And by the age of four, she should have had no more than two litters.

5. Are they willing to provide at least two client references, as well as contact information about their vet?

6. Do they question *you*—much like an adoption worker? Do they ask questions about your history and lifestyle? That's ideal! It shows how much the breeder cares about their pups.

7. Are they open and flexible about having you visit the pups on-site, first for an introductory meet-and-greet and perhaps once or twice before the pup turns eight weeks old?

Breeder Meet-and-Greet

Once all of you have passed this initial test, your breeder should be willing to provide a good mix of times and dates to facilitate and accommodate each meeting. Be wary of a breeder who allows visits only at one specific time. This could mean that they have to do a lot of prep work to make their facility appear clean, safe and well maintained. Don't fall for smoke and mirrors.

Once you've met the breeder and are ready to see the pups with their canine mom, look at this checklist of must-have factors and make sure the breeder meets all the requirements.

✓ The breeding pen should be clean, comfortable and warm.

✓ The mom should be with her pups, not separated from them.

✓ The mom and her pups should have access to outdoor space and the mom should have enough space and the ability to roam indoors and outdoors.

✓ The mom and any other adult dogs should appear friendly, healthy and well-balanced, not stressed and fearful of humans. This could show as aggressive tendencies (darting out at people and biting) or behaviours like obsessively running around in circles, cowering anxiously or urinating.

✓ Throughout the pups' first eight weeks, they should have had adequate socialization time with humans in steadily increasing increments of time. They should have ample time alone with the mom, especially during the first few weeks, but also a good dose of healthy exposure to humans, so that by the time you meet the pups, they're well acclimatized to our species.

✓ Both the mom and the pups should have a clean bill of health from the breeder's vet, and the breeder should know the pedigree of both the canine mom and the canine dad, along with the various health concerns and genetic illnesses that typically affect that specific breed. But be aware that many health issues don't become apparent for many months or even years, so you should focus on the health of the canine parents and understand that even an initial okay from a vet is no guarantee that your pup will not have future health issues.

✓ Avoid pups that have been isolated in a kennel for a long period of time. This could mean that the pup has already developed serious behavioural issues like separation anxiety and aggression.

✓ Make sure the breeder doesn't pressure you into making an initial down payment on the pup immediately. Everyone involved should be able to at least sleep on any decision, and ideally, you will all want to set up a second meeting before making a decision. You should also make your own independent trip to your own vet with the pup before you make a commitment to buy her.

✓ Even if the breeder checks out on all of the above, I strongly advise against purchasing two pups from the same litter. In fact, I think this is one of the biggest mistakes people make. Why? Because of the potential serious threat of dog pack competitiveness and interdog aggression, which is all too common, even with dogs from different litters, but especially with siblings from the same litter. This sibling rivalry tends to ramp up as the pups mature, from seemingly cute play fighting to attention-seeking manipulative behaviour to behavioural issues like digging and barking to outright aggression. Often, it's very challenging to identify which of the pups is the troublemaker. Many seemingly ideal siblings pups actually incite, bully and "egg on" bad behaviours among their brothers and sisters. If you must have sibling pups in your pack, wait until your first dog reaches maturity, at three years of age.

notes

1. Accessed June 1, 2011,
   http://www.pet-abuse.com/pages/cruelty_database.php
   http://www.pet-abuse.com/pages/cruelty_database/results.
   php?us_state=&ca_state=&uk_state=&nz_state=&au_
   state=&es_state=&animal_id%5B%5D=2&status=&month
   =&year=&gender=&keyword=&search=search
   http://www.pet-abuse.com/pages/cruelty_database/results.
   php?us_state=&ca_state=&uk_state=&nz_state=&au_
   state=&es_state=&animal_id%5B%5D=17&status=&month
   =&year=&gender=&keyword=&search=search
   http://www.pet-abuse.com/pages/cruelty_database/statistics/
   animals_by_cruelty_type.php
   http://www.pet-abuse.com/pages/cruelty_database/statistics/
   classifications.php.
2. Accessed July 12, 2011, http://www.humanesociety.org/issues/
   pet_overpopulation/.
3. Elizabeth M. Lund et al., "Prevalence and Risk Factors for
   Obesity in Adult Dogs from Private U.S. Veterinary
   Practices," *International Journal of Applied Research in
   Veterinary Medicine* 4 (2006): 177–86.
4. C. Schwab and L. Huber, "Obey or Not Obey? Dogs
   (Canis familiaris) Behave Differently in Response to
   Attentional States of their Owners," *Journal of Comparative
   Psychology* (August 2006): 169–75.

5. A. Haverbeke et al., "Training Methods of Military Dog Handlers and Their Effects on the Team's Performances," *Applied Animal Behaviour Science* 113 (2008): 110–22.

6. I.M. Bland et al., "Dog Obesity: Veterinary Practices' and Owners' Opinions on Cause and Management," *Preventive Veterinary Medicine* 94 (May 2010): 310–15.

7. I.M. Bland et al., "Dog Obesity: Owner Attitudes and Behaviour," *Preventive Veterinary Medicine* 92 (December 2009): 333–40.

8. Sherman et al., "Viewing Cute Images Increases Behavioral Carefulness," *Emotion* (April 2009): 282–86.

9. Sato Arai et al., "Importance of Bringing Dogs in Contact with Children during Their Socialization Period for Better Behavior," *Journal of Veterinary Medical Science* (June 2011): 747–52.

10. A. Haverbeke et al., "Training Methods of Military Dog Handlers and Their Effects on the Team's Performances," *Applied Animal Behaviour Science* 113 (2008): 110–22.

11. Lilla Tóth, Mórta Gácsi, Joózsef Topál and Adam Miklósi, "Playing Styles and Possible Causative Factors in Dogs' Behaviour When Playing with Humans," *Applied Animal Behaviour Science* 114 (2008): 473–84.

12. Z. Horváth, A Dóka and A. Miklósi, "Affiliative and Disciplinary Behavior of Human Handlers during Play with Their Dog Affects Cortisol Concentrations in Opposite Directions," *Hormones and Behavior* (June 2008): 107–14.

13. Martin Godbout and Diane Frank, "Excessive Mouthing in Puppies as a Predictor of Aggressiveness in Adult Dogs," *Journal of Veterinary Behavior: Clinical Applications and Research* (January 2011): 93.

14. V. Careau et al., "The Pace of Life under Artificial Selection: Personality, Energy Expenditure, and Longevity Are Correlated in Domestic Dogs," *The American Naturalist* 175/6 (June 2010): 753–58.

15. Chiara Mariti et al., "Puppies' Appeal for People: A Comparison with Small Adult Dogs," *Journal of Veterinary Behavior* 6 (January 2011): 89–90.

16. J. Topàl et al., "Attachment to Humans: A Comparative

Study on Hand-Reared Wolves and Differently Socialized Dog Puppies," *Animal Behavior* (December 2005): 1367–75.

17. J. Topál, Á. Miklósi and V. Csányi, "Dog–Human Relationship Affects Problem Solving Behavior in the Dog," *Anthrozoos* 10 (1997): 214–24.

18. Centers for Disease Control and Prevention, "Nonfatal Fall-Related Injuries Associated with Dogs and Cats — United States, 2001–2006," *Morbidity and Mortality Weekly Report* (March 2009): 277–81.

19. E.A. McCrave, "Diagnostic Criteria for Separation Anxiety in the Dog," *Veterinary Clinics of North America Small Animal Practice* (March 1991): 247–55.

20. G. Flannigan and N.H. Dodman, "Risk Factors and Behaviors Associated with Separation Anxiety in Dogs," *Journal of the American Veterinary Medical Association* (August 2001): 460–66.

21. Y. Takeuchi et al., "Differences in Background and Outcome of Three Behavior Problems of Dogs," *Applied Animal Behaviour Science* (January 2001): 297–308.

22. P.J. Holler et al., "Kinematic Motion Analysis of the Joints of the Forelimbs and Hind Limbs of Dogs during Walking Exercise Regimens," *American Journal of Veterinary Research* (July 2010) 71: 734–40.

23. Kate Ruder, "Brainy Border Collie Knows 200 Words," *Genome News Network* (June 2004). Accessed July 27, 2011, http://www. genomenewsnetwork.org/articles/2004/06/10/smartdog.php.

index

BRAD PATTISON is an animal trainer and human-being life coach who has been professionally reme-dying dog behaviour for almost 20 years. Best known for his TV series, *At the End of My Leash*, Pattison also founded Vancouver's Yuppy Puppy Dog Day Care Inc., pioneered the first Street Safety training program for dogs and facilitates courses that certify other dog trainers. His "6 Legs to Fitness" workout program for owners and their dogs has been featured on Discovery Channel's *Daily Planet*. During the Hurricane Katrina disaster, Pattison mobilized friends and created the Pattison Canine Rescue Team, which spent several weeks in Louisiana rescu-ing dogs from the floods. His previous book is *Brad Pattison Unleashed: A Dog's-Eye View of Life with Humans*. He lives in Kelowna.